the name of
JESUS

BOOKS BY KENNETH E. HAGIN

*Redeemed From Poverty, Sickness and Death
*What Faith Is
*Seven Vital Steps To Receiving the Holy Spirit
*Right and Wrong Thinking
 Prayer Secrets
*Authority of the Believer (foreign only)
*How To Turn Your Faith Loose
 The Key to Scriptural Healing
 The Ministry of a Prophet
 Praying To Get Results
 The Present-Day Ministry of Jesus Christ
 The Gift of Prophecy
 Healing Belongs to Us
 The Real Faith
*The Interceding Christian
 How You Can Know the Will of God
 Man on Three Dimensions
 The Human Spirit
 Turning Hopeless Situations Around
 Casting Your Cares Upon the Lord
 Seven Steps for Judging Prophecy
 The Origin and Operation of Demons
 Demons and How To Deal With Them
 Ministering to the Oppressed
 Bible Answers to Man's Questions on Demons
 Faith Food for Autumn
 Faith Food for Winter
 Faith Food for Spring
 Faith Food for Summer
*The New Birth
*Why Tongues?
*In Him
*God's Medicine
*You Can Have What You Say
 How To Write Your Own Ticket With God
*Don't Blame God
*Words
 Plead Your Case
*How To Keep Your Healing
 Laying on of Hands
 A Better Covenant
 Having Faith in Your Faith
 Five Hindrances to Growth in Grace
 Why Do People Fall Under the Power?
 The Bible Way To Receive the Holy Spirit
 Godliness Is Profitable
 I Went to Hell
 Three Big Words
 Obedience in Finances
 His Name Shall Be Called Wonderful
 Paul's Revelation: The Gospel of Reconciliation
 How To Walk in Love

The Precious Blood of Jesus
Love Never Fails
How God Taught Me About Prosperity
Learning To Forget
The Coming Restoration
New Thresholds of Faith
Prevailing Prayer to Peace
Concerning Spiritual Gifts
Bible Faith Study Course
Bible Prayer Study Course
The Holy Spirit and His Gifts
*The Ministry Gifts (Study Guide)
Seven Things You Should Know About Divine Healing
El Shaddai
Zoe: The God-Kind of Life
A Commonsense Guide to Fasting
Must Christians Suffer?
The Woman Question
The Believer's Authority
How You Can Be Led by the Spirit of God
What To Do When Faith Seems Weak and Victory Lost
The Name of Jesus
The Art of Intercession
Growing Up, Spiritually
Bodily Healing and the Atonement
Exceedingly Growing Faith
Understanding the Anointing
I Believe in Visions

BOOKS BY KENNETH HAGIN JR.

*Man's Impossibility — God's Possibility
Because of Jesus
The Key to the Supernatural
*Faith Worketh by Love
Blueprint for Building Strong Faith
*Seven Hindrances to Healing
*The Past Tense of God's Word
Healing: A Forever-Settled Subject
How To Make the Dream God Gave You Come True
Faith Takes Back What the Devil's Stolen
"The Prison Door Is Open — What Are You Still Doing Inside?"
Itching Ears
Where Do We Go From Here?
How To Be a Success in Life
Get Acquainted With God
Showdown With the Devil
Unforgiveness
The Answer for Oppression
Is Your Miracle Passing You By?
Commanding Power

*These titles are also available in Spanish. Information about other foreign translations of several of the above titles (i.e., Dutch, Finnish, French, German, Indonesian, Polish, Russian, Swahili, and Swedish) may be obtained by writing to: Kenneth Hagin Ministries, P.O. Box 50126, Tulsa, Oklahoma 74150-0126.

the name of
JESUS

Kenneth E. Hagin

Unless otherwise indicated, all Scripture quotations in this volume are from the *King James Version* of the Bible.

Fifth Printing 1986

ISBN 0-89276-502-X

In the U.S. write:
Kenneth Hagin Ministries
P.O. Box 50126
Tulsa, OK 74150-0126

In Canada write:
Kenneth Hagin Ministries
P.O. Box 335
Islington (Toronto), Ontario
Canada, M9A 4X3

Contents

1. The Name of Jesus 13

2. The More Excellent Name: How It Came 25

3. By Inheritance 27

4. By Bestowal 35

5. By Conquest 41

6. Authority in the Name 47

7. The Name: Possession of the Church 55

8. Backed by Deity 61

9. That Name—In Salvation 63

10. The Name and Baptisms 65

11. The Name of Jesus in our Daily Walk 71

12. All in the Name 77

13. In My Name Cast Out Demons 81

14. Can a Christian Be Possessed? 95

15. Three Necessary Steps 97

16. Wicked Spirits in the Heavenlies 101

17. In Him 105

18. The Miraculous! Christianity's Norm 113

19. Faith and the Name 117

20. Reigning by the Name 119

21. There Is Healing in the Name 121

22. Confession and the Name 135

23. Scriptures for Meditation 147

Preface

In February 1978, I taught our annual prayer seminar at RHEMA Bible Training Center in Tulsa. This is an open seminar; the public as well as the student body attends. One night the Lord very definitely spoke to me, as I was ministering to people in the healing line, about teaching a seminar on the Name of Jesus. That seminar has become this book.

At the time, I had one sermon I preached on this wonderful subject, but I had never really taught on it at length. I began to look around to see what I could find written on the subject. For others, you see, have revelations from God.

I was amazed at how little material there is in print on this subject. The only good book devoted entirely to it that I have found is E. W. Kenyon's *The Wonderful Name of Jesus*.[1] I encourage you to get a copy. It is a marvelous book. It is revelation knowledge. It is the Word of God.

Mr. Kenyon went home to be with the Lord in 1948. It was 1950 before I was introduced to his books. A brother in the Lord asked me, "Did you ever read after Dr. Kenyon?"

I said, "I've never heard of him."

He said, "You preach healing and faith just like he does."

He gave me some of Kenyon's books. And he did preach faith and healing just like I do. After all, if someone preaches the new birth, and somebody else preaches the new birth, it has to be the same. There is only one new birth. Likewise, if you preach faith and healing—and I mean Bible-faith and Bible-healing—it has to be the same. We may have different ways to express it, but if it is according to the Word of God, it is the same truth.

I began then to check up on Mr. Kenyon's life. The Bible teaches that we should take as examples those *"who through faith and patience inherit the promises"* (Heb. 6:12). I like to see if a man lives what he teaches.

Some people seem to want to find somebody the Bible didn't work for to set up as an example. They always talk about somebody who didn't receive their healing. Well, in preaching salvation, you don't talk about someone who didn't get saved. No, you talk about those who did get saved. You don't encourage Christians to follow the example of those who backslide. You talk about people who walk in the light of God's Word and enjoy His blessings.

I like to check up on people. I like to follow those who inherit the promises. That's why I teach those training for the ministry at RHEMA Bible Training Center each year from F. F. Bosworth's book, *Christist the Healer.*[2] I was personally acquainted with Bosworth. The last time I was in one of his meetings, he was 77. At 80-some-odd years of age, he announced one day, "This is the greatest day of my life. God has shown me that I'm going home." He called in a friend for a time of visiting. Then he went home.

Kenyon, too, went home to be with the Lord without sickness and disease at the age of nearly 81. He was holding Bible classes in Southern California shortly before his death, teaching several times a day. (His daughter, Ruth Housworth, who keeps his ministry and writings going stronger today than ever, said that the young people in the team which traveled with him had a difficult time keeping up with his pace.) He had just finished writing *The Hidden Man of the Heart*.[3] And he came home to rest for a while. One morning his wife and daughter asked what he would like for breakfast. He replied, "You girls go ahead and eat. I don't believe I will eat right now." A short time later he was home with the Lord. He went home the Bible way without sickness or disease.

In the Name of Jesus seminar I conducted in April 1978, I quoted freely from E. W. Kenyon's book, *The Wonderful Name of Jesus*. I particularly like the way he grouped the Scriptures for study. I like his outline. I acknowledge here my deep appreciation for the revelation knowledge God gave him on this wonderful Name, for his willingness and obedience to teach and live it. I also want to express special appreciation to Ruth Housworth, for her dedication in getting the message out in print, and for granting us permission to quote from his book in this book for the edification of the body of Christ, to the glory of God the Father.

[1] E. W. Kenyon, *The Wonderful Name of Jesus*, Lynnwood, Washington, Kenyon's Gospel Publishing Society.

[2] F. F. Bosworth, *Christ the Healer*, Old Tappan, New Jersey, Fleming H. Revell.

[3] E. W. Kenyon, *The Hidden Man of the Heart*, Lynnwood, Washington, Kenyon's Gospel Publishing Society.

Chapter 1
The Name of Jesus

E. W. Kenyon began his book *The Wonderful Name of Jesus* with this personal account:

> One afternoon, while giving an address on "The Name of Jesus" a lawyer interrupted me, asking:
>
> "Do you mean to say that Jesus gave us the 'Power of Attorney' the Legal Right to use His Name?"
>
> I said to him, "Brother, you are a lawyer and I am a layman. Tell me—did Jesus give us the 'Power of Attorney?' "
>
> He said, "If language means anything, then Jesus gave the church the Power of Attorney."
>
> Then I asked him, "What is the value of this Power of Attorney?"
>
> He answered, "It depends upon how much there is back of it, how much authority, how much power this Name represents."
>
> Then I began to search to find how much power and authority Jesus had.

All the power, and all the authority that Jesus had is invested in His Name!

The question is: Do we have the power of attorney to use His Name?

The Word of God teaches that we do. Jesus said we could use His Name in prayer. He said we could use His Name in dealing with demons. He said we could use His Name in ministering healing.

In fact, that's where the secret lies—in the use of that Name! We have depended, too much of the time, on our own ability to deliver someone—when in reality, it is the Name that does it.

13

Kenyon wrote:

> The measure of His ability [the measure of the ability of
> the Lord Jesus Christ] is the measure of the value of that
> Name, and all that is invested in that Name belongs to us,
> for Jesus gave us the unqualified use of His Name.

The Name in Prayer

Jesus said, in regard to the use of His Name in prayer:

JOHN 16:24
**24 Hitherto have ye asked nothing IN MY NAME: ask,
and ye shall receive, that your joy may be full.**

Hitherto means *up till now*, or *till this time.* In other
words, up till the time that Jesus was speaking here to the
disciples, they had asked nothing in His Name.

Now He is speaking to them about a "new day" upon
the earth, and He is telling them, *"Ask and ye shall receive,
that your joy may be full."*

No, we do not ask for Jesus' sake. Asking for Jesus'
sake is not asking in His Name. We are asking for our own
sake. It isn't Jesus who needs healing: it is we who need
healing. It isn't Jesus who needs an answer to prayer. We
do. Due to a lack of knowledge along this line, many
prayers have been destroyed and have not worked because
they were prayed for Jesus' sake, instead of in Jesus'
Name.

Here in John, Jesus not only gives us the use of His
Name in New Covenant prayer, but He also declares that
the prayer prayed in His Name will receive His special
attention:

JOHN 16:23
23 . . . Verily, verily, I say unto you, Whatsoever ye
shall ask the Father IN MY NAME, he will give it you.

Notice what Jesus is saying: You ask of the Father in
My Name—I will endorse it—and the Father will give it to
you.

What an amazing prayer promise! Yet because we did
not understand what Jesus said, and because we were
religiously brainwashed instead of New Testament
taught, we watered down the promises of God. We tacked
on something Jesus did not say. We added something else
to it. "God will, *if it is His will*—but it might not be His
will," we have said.

You don't find that kind of talk in the New Testament.
People have gone along without answers to prayer, saying,
"It must not have been His will, because He didn't do it. If
it had been His will, He would have done it."

Jesus stated God's will here in John 16:23,24.

I was born again the 22nd day of April 1933. When I
was born again, I was on the bed of sickness and
helplessness. It was there that I learned some of the
secrets of prayer and the use of the Name of Jesus I am
sharing here. It took me a while to learn—I was bedfast 16
months—but in August 1934, I learned to pray the prayer
of faith and received my healing.

Now I am going to say something, and I want you to pay
close attention to how I say it. (Some people grab hold of
part of what you say and miss the whole of it.) Understand
that when it comes to praying about someone else, their
will comes in on the situation. Nobody, through prayer
and faith, can push something off on someone else which
that person does not want. If we could, we would all put

salvation off on everybody, wouldn't we? When it comes to praying for the other fellow, about his needs, and about his requests, his will comes in—and his doubt can nullify the effects of my faith. Another person's unbelief, however, cannot affect my prayers for my needs.

Now with that word of explanation, this is what I wanted to say. *I have not prayed one prayer in 45 years* (I'm talking about for me and for my children while they were young) *without getting an answer.* I always got an answer—and the answer was always yes.

Some people say, "God always answers prayers. Sometimes He says, 'Yes,' and sometimes He says, 'No'."

I never read that in the Bible. That is just human reasoning.

Jesus did not say, "Hitherto ye have asked nothing in my name: ask, and ye shall receive; however, sometimes He will say, 'No,' and sometimes He will say, 'Yes,' and sometimes He will say, 'Wait a while.' "

We have added such as that to the Bible trying to give people an answer as to why prayer hasn't worked for them. Yet the reason it has not worked for them is, they did not work the Word. If it did not work for me, it would be because I was not in line with the Word.

A person can be a good Christian, sanctified, separated, and holy, and still not get the job done when it comes to answered prayer. We believe in people living right, but you cannot come bragging on yourself when you come to pray. You cannot come to the throne of grace, telling God what all you've done, bragging about that, and get an answer.

No! We come bringing the Name of Jesus! And God's Word works today, just as much as it ever did.

"Ask the Father *in My Name*," Jesus said. "I will

endorse that, and the Father will give it to you."

Kenyon says:

> This puts prayer on a purely legal basis for He has given us the legal right to use His Name.
>
> As we take our privileges, and rights, in the New Covenant and pray in Jesus' Name, it passes out of our hands into the hands of Jesus; He then assumes the responsibility of that prayer, and we know that He said, "Father, I thank Thee that Thou hearest Me, and I know that Thou hearest Me always."
>
> In other words, we know that the Father always hears Jesus, and when we pray in Jesus' Name, it is as though Jesus Himself were doing the praying—He takes our place.
>
> This places prayer not only on legal grounds, but makes it a business proposition.
>
> When we pray, we take Jesus' place here to carry out His will, and He takes our place before the Father.

The Name in Combat

The Name of Jesus is to be used in combat against the unseen forces that surround us. We have authority in the Name of Jesus against all powers of darkness.

MARK 16:17,18
17 And these signs shall follow them that believe; IN MY NAME shall they cast out devils; they shall speak with new tongues;
18 They shall take up serpents; and if they drink any deadly thing, it shall not hurt them; they shall lay hands on the sick, and they shall recover.

Another translation says, *"These signs shall accompany . . . . "* I like that. Somebody following you is going along behind you, but somebody accompanying you is going right along with you. This translation agrees with

the Scripture that says we are workers together with Him
(2 Cor. 6:1).

Literally, in the Greek, Mark 16:17 says, *"These signs
shall accompany the believing ones; IN MY NAME shall
they . . . . "* Every child of God is a believing one. Since
these signs are done *"IN MY NAME,"* they must belong to
every child of God, because the Name of Jesus belongs to
every child of God.

*"IN MY NAME shall they cast out devils; they shall
speak with new tongues . . . .* [We have the right to speak
with tongues in the Name of Jesus!] *They shall take up
serpents; and if they drink any deadly thing, it shall not
hurt them; they shall lay hands on the sick, and they shall
recover."*

"Here," Kenyon says, "Jesus is revealing His part in
the Great Commission." Let's look at that great document
in Matthew:

> **MATTHEW 28:18-20**
> **18 And Jesus came and spake unto them, saying, All
> power [authority] is given unto me in heaven and in
> earth.**
> **19 Go ye therefore, and teach all nations, baptizing
> them in the name of the Father, and of the Son, and of
> the Holy Ghost:**
> **20 Teaching them to observe all things whatsoever I
> have commanded you: and, lo, I am with you alway,
> even unto the end of the world.**

The King James translation reads that Jesus said, *"All
power . . . . "* More than one Greek word is translated
power in the New Testament. W. E. Vine's *Expository
Dictionary of New Testament Words*[1] shows that the Greek
word translated *power* here is a word most often translated
authority. Many translations read that way.

Jesus said, *"All AUTHORITY is given unto me in heaven and in earth."*

Now, if you stop reading right there, you might rejoice saying, "Thank God, Jesus has the authority. He has the authority in heaven and in earth. He can do whatever He wants to do. It is up to Him, because He has it."

But that is not all Jesus said. Immediately, He authorized the Church to go forth in His Name! *"All authority in given unto me in heaven and in earth. GO YE THEREFORE . . . . "!*

One minister wrote me after I had appeared on "The 700 Club" television program. He was always taught to believe that if God wants to do it, He does it. He has the authority—He has the power—just leave it up to God. There was sickness in this minister's home. There was mental depression in his own life. He just accepted that the Lord was working out something. So he went along in the ministry for years, depressed and oppressed himself, sickness and disease in his family. He'd had no victory in his life for years.

"But," he wrote, "God already had been dealing with me—and I guess I was just ready to hear what you said."

God was trying to bring the truth to his spirit, that it is not so much up to God, concerning matters on this earth, as it is up to us.

He wrote, "When you began to say some things, I got my eyes opened. I began to see. It seemed like the Lord spoke to my heart and said, 'That's what I've been trying to tell you all the time.' "

(Because our heads have been educated a certain way, it is sometimes difficult for us to listen to our hearts.)

"I'm beginning to see," he said, "that it is up to us to do something about some of these situations which exist—

that he has authorized us to do it."

When you sum it up, this is what Jesus said, "All authority has been given unto me in heaven and in earth. Now I am authorizing you. I am sending you out to make disciples of all nations . . . And, lo, I am with you always . . . . "

How is He with us?

Let's go back to the 18th chapter of Matthew.

> **MATTHEW 18:19**
> **19 Again I say unto you, That if two of you shall agree on earth as touching any thing that they shall ask, it shall be done for them of my Father which is in heaven.**

Now that's a wonderful verse. That's a wonderful statement of fact. But I think we miss what Jesus is saying by lifting that verse out of context and quoting it alone, because He gives the reason, the secret, of why it will be done in the next verse:

> **MATTHEW 18:20**
> **20 For where two or three are gathered together IN MY NAME, there am I in the midst of them.**

Hallelujah!

Now again, when we take this 20th verse and lift it out of context and quote it alone, what we are saying is true all right, but we leave the impression that is the full import of the verse.

An example of this is when we come together in a church service and say, "The Lord is here because He said, 'Where two or three are gathered together in My Name, I am there.' "

That is true, in a sense, but that is not really what He is talking about in this verse. He is not talking about a church service. He is talking about those two on earth who are agreeing. He is telling why it is going to work for the two of them, or even a third.

"Again I say unto you, That if two of you shall agree on earth as touching any thing that they shall ask, it shall be done for them of my Father which is in heaven. FOR where two or three are gathered together IN MY NAME, there am I in the midst of them."

There am I! **He is right there to see to it that what those two or three agreed upon comes to pass!**

Now let's go back again to the 28th chapter of Matthew where He said, *"Lo, I am with you alway."*

How is He with us?

Well, He said that where those two or three people agree as touching anything they ask, *"IN MY NAME, THERE AM I in the midst of them."*

That is the secret. **He is with us in the power, and in the authority of His Name!**

The Resources of Jesus

E. W. Kenyon makes these powerful statements, and then issues a thrilling challenge to the Church:

> When Jesus gave us the legal right to use this Name, the Father knew all that that Name would imply when breathed in prayer . . . and it is His joy to recognize that Name.
>
> So the possibilities enfolded in that Name are beyond our understanding, and when He says to the Church, "Whatsoever ye shall ask of the Father in My Name," He is giving us a signed check on the resources of heaven and

asking us to fill it in.

It would pay the Church to begin an exhaustive study of the resources of Jesus in order to get a measurement of the wealth that Name holds for her today.

Christians are where they are in life because they have written their own ticket, or their own check, so to speak, to arrive there. Most have written small checks because they had a small vision of Jesus and of that Name.

A few times, when it was necessary, I have signed my name on a check and let somebody else fill it in. Of course, I did instruct them how to fill it in. I did not want them writing in just anything. But what Jesus has done is this: He has signed a check and turned it over to us.

Too many people have filled it in for one dollar— thinking they were being humble—when they ought to have filled it in for one hundred thousand dollars. Therefore they have lived on a low level of life.

Jesus has given pastors of local congregations, for instance, this check, saying, "You just fill it in." So they filled it in for a few dollars, and for 25 years they've been located in a rundown building which brings disgrace to the Name of Jesus. Is that all His Name could provide?

In individual lives, the same thing is true. Many born-again, Spirit-filled Christians live on a low level of life, overcome by the devil. In fact, they talk more about the devil than anything else. Every time they give a hard luck story, they're bragging on the devil. Every time they talk about how sick they are, they're bragging on the devil. (He is the author of sickness and disease—not God.) Every time they say, "It doesn't look like we're going to make it," they are bragging on the devil.

No, let's talk about Jesus! Let's talk about the Name of Jesus!

He gave us, individually, a signed check, saying, "Fill it in." He gave us a signed check on the resources of heaven.

It would change our lives to make an exhaustive study of the resources of Jesus in order to get a measurement of the wealth that Name holds for the Church and for every believer today.

If we have a low estimation and a low respect for the Name, we will not expect much, because we do not know what belongs to us.

[1] W. E. Vine, *An Expository Dictionary of New Testament Words*, Old Tappan, New Jersey, Fleming H. Revell, p. 89.

Chapter 2
The More Excellent Name:
How It Came

Kenyon points out that men obtain great names in three ways. Some men are born to a great name—a king, for instance. Others make their name great by their achievements. Still others have a great name conferred upon them.

The more excellent Name came by all three means. Jesus' Name is great because He inherited a great Name. His Name is great because of His achievements. His Name is great because it was conferred upon Him.

We are about to examine these marvelous truths in depth. They are almost beyond our capacity to grasp. But as we feed upon them, little by little they will become a part of our inner consciousness. We need to catch a glimpse of them in our spirits—not in our heads. (Yet they do have to go through our heads to get down into our hearts; the mind is the door to the heart.) Once these truths really dawn on our hearts, it will be said of us as it was in the Old Testament, "There are giants in the land." For this will make us to become spiritual giants!

Some of us have caught a glimpse occasionally—and we have done exploits. But by continuing to feed along this line, I believe we can get to the place where we won't just visit there occasionally—but we will live in this place.

Chapter 3
By Inheritance

"God, who at sundry times and in divers manners spake in time past unto the fathers by the prophets, Hath in these last days spoken unto us by his Son, whom he hath appointed heir of all things, by whom also he made the worlds; Who being the brightness of his glory, and the express image of his person, and upholding all things by the word of his power, when he had by himself purged our sins, sat down on the right hand of the Majesty on high; Being made so much better than the angels, as he hath BY INHERITANCE obtained a MORE EXCELLENT NAME than they.

For unto which of the angels said he at any time, Thou art my son, this day have I begotten thee? And again, I will be to him a Father, and he shall be to me a Son? And again, when he bringeth in the firstbegotten into the world, he saith, And let all the angels of God worship him."

—Hebrews 1:1-6

Jesus inherited a *"more excellent name than they."* He inherited a greater Name than any angelic being.

As Son, He is heir of all things.

He is *"the express image"* of God. He is *"the brightness,"* or as one translation reads, *"the outshining,"* of the Father.

He is God speaking to us.

And He *"by inheritance obtained a more excellent name."*

When did He inherit it?

He did not inherit anything in heaven before He came to this earth, because He already had everything.

He did not inherit it when He came to the earth, because the Epistle to the Philippians says that He stripped Himself of all honor and glory.

When did He inherit His Name? There is a clue in the following verses:

> **HEBREWS 1:4,5**
> **4 Being made so much better than the angels, as he hath by inheritance obtained a more excellent name than they.**
> **5 For unto which of the angels said he at any time, Thou art my son, this day have I begotten thee? . . . .**

These verses tell us *when* He inherited this more excellent Name. It was when God said to Him, "*Thou art my son, THIS DAY have I begotten thee.*" This day! That's when it happened—the day He was begotten.

When was Jesus begotten?

Most people think He was begotten when He came into the world as the Babe of Bethlehem.

No! Oh, no! Begotten means born. The Son of God was not born as He took on flesh. He preexisted with the Father. He just took upon Himself a body.

> **HEBREWS 10:5**
> **5 Wherefore when he cometh into the world he saith, Sacrifice and offering thou wouldest not, but a body hast thou prepared me.**

He was not begotten when he came into the world; He always preexisted with the Father. (My remarks are in brackets in the following Scripture.)

JOHN 1:1,14
1 In the beginning was the Word, and the Word was with God, and the Word was God.
14 And the Word [which already existed, and did not need to be begotten, or born] was made flesh, and dwelt among us . . . .

No, *"Thou art my son, THIS DAY have I begotten thee,"* is not talking about the day He took upon Himself a body. Then what day was it?

ACTS 13:33
33 God hath fulfilled the same unto us their children, in that HE HATH RAISED UP JESUS AGAIN; as it is also written in the second psalm, THOU ART MY SON, THIS DAY HAVE I BEGOTTEN THEE.

When was it that Jesus was begotten? When He was raised up! On that Resurrection morn!

Why did He need to be begotten, or born? Because He became like we were, separated from God. Because He tasted spritual death for every man. His spirit, His inner man, went to hell in our place.

HEBREWS 2:9
9 But we see Jesus, who was made a little lower than the angels for the suffering of death, crowned with glory and honour; that he by the grace of God should taste death for every man.

Physical death would not remove our sins. He tasted death for every man—spiritual death.

Jesus is the first person ever to be born again. Why did His spirit need to be born again? Because it was estranged from God. Do you remember how He cried out on the cross, "My God, my God, why hast thou forsaken me?"

Many people do not know what the Bible means when it talks about death. Death, in the Bible, never means the cessation of existence. Never!

Several kinds of deaths are spoken of in the Bible, but there are three kinds with which we need to familiarize ourselves: (1) spiritual death; (2) physical death; (3) eternal death (or, the second death—being cast into the lake which burneth with fire and brimstone).

What is spiritual death? It is the opposite of spiritual Life. It does not mean the cessation of being.

Ephesians 2:1 says, *"And you WHO WERE DEAD in trespasses and sins"*—that's us before we were born again— *"hath He quickened."* Quickened means made alive. (See Eph. 2:5.)

Paul wrote to Timothy and talked about some people being dead while they live (1 Tim. 5:6). He did not mean they had ceased to exist.

When we talk about a sinner's being in spiritual death, we do not mean his spirit does not exist. His spirit does exist, and will exist eternally, because that part of man— whether he is saved or unsaved—is like God. Man is an eternal spirit. (He possesses a soul.) But the sinner's spirit is not in fellowship, and not in relationship with God.

God told Adam, concerning the tree of the knowledge of good and evil, *"Thou shalt not eat of it: for in the day that thou eatest thereof thou shalt surely die"* (Gen. 2:17).

He had no reference to physical death, because Adam did not die that day, physically. But the moment he ate of it, he did die, *spiritually*. That does not mean that Adam ceased to exist. It means he immediately was out of fellowship and out of relationship with God.

Adam had been walking and talking with God, in fellowship, in relationship to Him. This time, when God came down in the cool of the day to commune and fellowship with him, Adam was nowhere to be found. He called out to him, "Adam, where art thou?" Adam answered, "*I was afraid . . . and I hid myself.*" Why? Because he had sinned.

Sin separates from God. **Spiritual death means separation from God.** The moment Adam sinned, he was separated from God.

Spiritual death means something more than separation from God. **Spiritual death also means having Satan's nature.** Jesus said to the Pharisees, "*Ye are of your father the devil, and the lusts of your father ye will do. He was a murderer from the beginning, and abode not in the truth, because there is no truth in him. When he speaketh a lie, he speaketh of his own: for he is a liar, and the father of it*" (John 8:44). The Pharisees were very religious. They went to the synagogue on the Sabbath, they prayed, they paid their tithes, they fasted, and they did a lot of other fine and good things—but they lied about Christ and murdered Him. Jesus said they were children of the devil—they had the characteristics of the devil.

When one is born again, he takes upon himself the nature of God—which is Life and peace. The nature of the devil is hatred and lies.

Jesus tasted death—spiritual death—for every man. Sin is more than a physical act; it is a spiritual act. He became what we were, that we might become what He is.

2 CORINTHIANS 5:21
21 For he hath made him to be sin for us, who knew no sin; that we might be made the righteousness of God in him.

Jesus became sin. His spirit was separated from God. And He went down into hell in our place.

Notice in the following Scripture, that Peter, preaching on the day of Pentecost concerning the Lord Jesus Christ, said, *"Thou wilt not leave my soul in hell, neither wilt thou suffer thine Holy One to see corruption."* I encourage you to read Peter's entire message. He brings out the fact that David, in Psalm 16:8-10, was really prophesying by the Spirit of God.

> **ACTS 2:25-27; 29-31**
> **25 For David speaketh concerning him, I foresaw the Lord always before my face, for he is on my right hand, that I should not be moved:**
> **26 Therefore did my heart rejoice, and my tongue was glad; moreover also my flesh shall rest in hope:**
> **27 Because thou wilt not leave my soul in hell, neither wilt thou suffer thine Holy One to see corruption . . . .**
> **29 Men and brethren, let me freely speak unto you of the patriarch David, that he is both dead and buried, and his sepulchre is with us unto this day.**
> **30 Therefore being a prophet, and knowing that God had sworn with an oath to him, that of the fruit of his loins, according to the flesh, he would raise up Christ to sit on his throne;**
> **31 He seeing this before spake of the resurrection of Christ, that his soul was not left in hell, neither his flesh did see corruption.**

Paul is talking about the same thing in Acts 13:33.

> **ACTS 13:33**
> **33 God hath fulfilled the same unto us their children, in that he hath raised up Jesus again; as it is also written in the second psalm, Thou art my Son, this day have I begotten thee.**

It is clear that both Peter and Paul are talking about the same thing.

You will not be able to understand the authority in the Name of Jesus until you understand this fact. Down in the prison house of suffering—down in hell itself—Jesus satisfied the claims of Justice on the behalf of each one of us, because He died as our substitute.

God in heaven said, "It is enough." Then he raised Him up. He brought His spirit and soul up out of hell—He raised His body up from the grave—and He said, "Thou art my son, THIS DAY have I begotten thee."

What day? The day He was begotten. The day He was raised up.

That's the day, then, that He hath by inheritance obtained a more excellent Name!

Chapter 4

By Bestowal

"Wherefore God also hath highly exalted him, and GIVEN HIM A NAME WHICH IS ABOVE EVERY NAME: That at the name of Jesus every knee should bow, of things [beings] in heaven, and things [beings] in earth, and things [beings] under the earth; And that every tongue should confess that Jesus Christ is Lord, to the glory of God the Father."

—Philippians 2:9-11

God gave Him a Name, which is above every Name. E. W. Kenyon writes:

> The inference is that there was a Name known in heaven, unknown elsewhere, and this Name was kept to be conferred upon some one who should merit it: and Jesus, as we know Him—the Eternal Son as He is known in the bosom of the Father—was given this Name, and at this Name every knee shall bow in the three worlds—Heaven, Earth, and Hell—and every tongue shall confess that He is Lord of the three worlds to the glory of God, the Father.

Paul was praying a prayer for the Church at Ephesus in the first chapter of Ephesians. He wanted them to see something—to understand something. So he prayed that the eyes of their spirit would be enlightened to truths they would never be able to figure out in their heads. This is his Spirit-inspired and anointed prayer:

> *"That the God of our Lord Jesus Christ, the Father of glory, may give unto you the spirit of wisdom and revelation*

in the knowledge of him:

"The eyes of your understanding being enlightened; that ye may know what is the hope of his calling, and what the riches of the glory of his inheritance in the saints,

"And what is the exceeding greatness of his power to usward who believe, according to the working of his mighty power,

"Which he wrought in Christ, WHEN HE RAISED HIM FROM THE DEAD, and set him at his own right hand in the heavenly places,

"Far above all principality, and power, and might, and dominion, AND EVERY NAME THAT IS NAMED, not only in this world, but also in that which is to come:

"And hath put all things under his feet, and gave him to be the head over all things to the church,

"Which is his body, the fulness of him that filleth all in all."

—Ephesians 1:17-23

Notice that in connection with His being raised from the dead, the Name is mentioned.

Paul's prayer was not for the Church at Ephesus only. Because this is a Spirit-given prayer, it belongs to believers everywhere—here in Tulsa, where I live, and wherever you live. It belongs to us.

It is a prayer that the eyes of our spirits might be enlightened to some things. (That is where we have to get the knowledge of God's Word—in our spirits, our hearts, down on the inside. We cannot get it with our mentality—our mentality is not great enough to grasp it.) God wants us to know some things, to see some things, to be enlightened to some things in our hearts. Here is Moffatt's translation of that prayer.

May the God of our Lord Jesus Christ, the glorious Father, grant you the Spirit of wisdom and revelation for the knowledge of himself, illuminating the eyes of your heart so that you can understand the hope to which He calls us, the wealth of his glorious heritage in the saints, and the surpassing greatness of his power over us believers—a power which operates with the strength of the might which he exerted in raising Christ from the dead and seating him at his right hand in the heavenly sphere, above all the angelic rulers, authorities, powers, and lords, above every name that is to be named not only in this age—but in the age to come— he has put everything under his feet and set him as head over everything FOR THE CHURCH, the church which is his Body, filled by him who fills the universe entirely.

God not only gave him a Name before which every being in the three worlds must bow and confess His lordship, but God seated Him in the highest place in the universe, at His own right hand, and made Him to be head over all things.

For what purpose?

FOR THE CHURCH! For the benefit of the Church (v.22)! Kenyon writes:

> God has made this investment for the benefit of the Church; He has made this deposit on which the Church has a right to draw for Her every need.
>
> He has given to Him the Name that has within it the fullness of the Godhead, the wealth of the Eternities, and the love of the heart of the Father-God: and, that Name is given us.
>
> We have the right to use that Name against our enemies.
>
> We have the right to use it in our petitions.
>
> We have the right to use it in our praises and worship.
>
> That Name has been given unto us.

It belongs to us!

Heaven, earth, and hell recognize what Jesus did. All that Jesus did, all the authority, all the power, all of His achievements are in His Name. And the Name on our lips will work the same things now as it did then.

The last week of August 1952, I was holding a meeting in East Texas. I was lying across my bed one afternoon, with my Bible and another book, doing some studying. I was not necessarily studying for the service that night, but just feeding upon God's Word for my own spiritual edification and benefit.

One of the Scriptures I was looking at was Philippians 2:9,10 about the Name of Jesus, and how, at the Name of Jesus, beings in heaven, and in earth, and under the earth, must bow.

Momentarily, I caught a glimpse of something—in my spirit, not in my natural mind. I caught a glimpse, just momentarily, of the Name of Jesus—and the authority of that Name—what that Name would do—and particularly about "*in the earth.*" You know, that's where we're living—right here on the earth.

That Name will work in heaven; it will work here on the earth; it will work under the earth. It will work in all three worlds. And those are the three worlds with which we have to do.

I can remember how on that afternoon, with that revelation in my spirit—though just a glimpse—I rose up! I *knew* that Name worked! I said, "In the Name of Jesus! In the Name of Jesus! In the Name of Jesus, I break the power of the devil over my brother Dub's life. I claim his deliverance. I claim his salvation."

To me that settled it. Within 10 days, he was born again. I had prayed and fasted for him off and on for 15 years, which never seemed to do any good. But the minute

I rose up with the Name of Jesus, it worked!

It will not work for you, however, until you get the revelation of it. And you will not get the revelation of it without studying. I was studying, feeding on God's Word. This is why I am teaching along this line. You may not get the revelation of what I am saying just now, but if you will continue to feed, continue to study, sooner or later—now if you throw it away or give it up, it won't ever happen to you—what the Word of God is saying will dawn on your heart, on your spirit, down on the inside of you.

I do not think these truths have registered upon our spirit consciousness. I do not think the church world as a whole knows anything at all about it. We use the Name, but just as we do any other name. We do not realize the significance of it. We do not realize the authority of it. Yet He gave us the right to use the Name that was given to Him.

Chapter 5

By Conquest

In Paul's prayer for the Church, he stated that God had raised Christ from the dead, and set Him at His own right hand in the heavenlies, *"Far above all principality, and power, and might, and dominion, and every name that is named . . . . "* (Eph. 1:20,21).

By His *conquest* of these principalities, powers, mights, and dominions, Jesus obtained that Name!

> **COLOSSIANS 2:15**
> 15 And having spoiled principalities and powers, he made a shew of them openly, triumphing over them in it.

Another translation says, *"He PUT TO NOUGHT principalities and powers, making a show of them openly, triumphing over them in it."* Another translation says, He *"paralyzed"* them. These are the same principalities and powers spoken of in Ephesians 6:12:

> **EPHESIANS 6:12**
> 12 For we wrestle not against flesh and blood, but against principalities, against powers, against the rulers of the darkness of this world, against spiritual wickedness in high places.

The principalities and powers we wrestle against are the same ones that He overcame, that He spoiled, that He put to nought. Put to nought means, reduced to nothing! As far as we are concerned, He reduced them to nothing! No wonder He said, "In my Name they will cast out demons"!

Jesus met Satan and his cohorts on their own territory

and defeated them. The conquest that Jesus made of the devil, of sin, of sickness and disease is wrapped up in the Name. And the Name belongs to us. The Name, when we use it, will bring into reality in our lives what Jesus has already accomplished. I think that's the reason the devil has fought so hard to keep us from knowing about it.

You can just repeat the Name, like a parrot saying, "Polly wants a cracker," and it won't do a thing for you. But oh, when you know what is back of that Name—when you know the authority invested in that Name—when you know what Jesus wrought, and that He arose on that glad Resurrection morning—when you know that He said, "All authority is given unto me, in heaven and in earth. **Go ye therefore** .... I'm giving you My Name. I'm giving you authority. Go in My Name"—HALLELUJAH! Let's take that Name!

> COLOSSIANS 1:13
> 13 Who hath delivered us from the power [authority] of darkness, and hath translated us into the kingdom of his dear Son.

It was in His spoiling the principalities and powers, putting them to nought, overcoming them, defeating them, that He delivered us from the "power of darkness." That means from the power, or authority, of Satan.

Satan has no authority to dominate the Christian or the Church.

When you know this truth, and know that the Name belongs to you, you can put Satan on the run every time. I mean every single time!

Some people say to me, "Well, I tried that and it didn't work."

I always tell them, "If you will repent for lying, God

will forgive you."

God has delivered us from the power of darkness, from the authority of darkness, from the authority of Satan, from the authority of Satan's kingdom—and He has translated us into the kingdom of His dear Son!

I want to show you something that will corroborate what I have been teaching. First, let's look at First Corinthians 2:6 in the King James translation.

1 CORINTHIANS 2:6
6 Howbeit we speak wisdom among them that are perfect [mature]: yet not the wisdom of this world, nor of the princes of this world, that come to nought.

Let's look at that same verse in Moffatt's translation:

1 CORINTHIANS 2:6 *(Moffatt)*
6 We do discuss 'wisdom' with those who are mature; only it is not the wisdom of this world or of the dethroned Powers who rule this world.

The King James translation speaks of the *"princes of this world, that come to nought."* Moffatt's translation calls them *"the dethroned Powers who rule this world."*

Consider First Corinthians 2:6 in the light of Colossians 2:15 and you will see that it was when Jesus spoiled principalities and powers, making a show of them openly, triumphing over them in it, that they were brought to nought and dethroned.

Why then is the devil—depression, oppression, demons, sickness, and everything else that is of the devil— ruling so many Christians and even churches?

It is because they do not know what belongs to them.

They take the Name of Jesus like you would take a good-luck charm: "If I carry this rabbit's foot, maybe it will keep something from happening." They seem to think like this, "If I take the Name of Jesus it might work."

No! Find out all the authority that is back of that Name. Know that as far as God is concerned, and as far as the believer is concerned, these rulers, these princes of this world are dethroned. Jesus dethroned them.

They are not *going to be* dethroned—they are dethroned.

"Well," some people say, "we know that during the Millennium they will be dethroned."

No! He's already done it! We are in the world, but we are not of the world—they have no right to rule us.

In teaching on divine healing and health, I have often said, "I haven't had a headache in so-many years." (At this writing it has been 45 years.)

I guess the devil got tired of hearing me say it. Just a few months ago, as I left the office building and started home, suddenly my head started hurting.

(Someone might say, "Well, you had a headache." No, I didn't have one! I don't have headaches. I haven't had a headache since August 1934.)

Then, as if someone were sitting in the back seat—and of course, the devil was there, but he doesn't bother me because I know he's put to nought—I heard these words, "Ah ha! You've got a headache."

I said, "In the Name of Jesus (*You see, the Name stands for all of His authority and power!*), I do not have a headache. In the Name of Jesus, I will not have a headache. And in the Name of Jesus, pain, you leave."

I hadn't gotten the words out of my mouth, until it left. It just disappeared.

Someone said, "I wish I could get that to work for me."

It does not work by wishing—it works by knowing.

The reason for this book is to get people to know. Do not forget the Scriptures we use. Look them up. Study them. Feed on them until they become a part of your inner consciousness. That's when they start working for you.

Oh, there is a Name that's above every Name—the Name of Jesus. Heaven, earth, and hell realize what that Name means. We need to realize it.

No wonder Mr. Kenyon called his book *The Wonderful Name of Jesus*. That Name is just as wonderful as He is. That Name is just as mighty as He is. That Name is just as powerful as He is. That Name is just as great as He is. That's the reason it is a more excellent Name.

Think about the excellency of Jesus—His Name is just as excellent.

Think about Jesus being above all—above all dominion, above all power, above all principalities, and every name that is named—so is His Name!

Meditate on that! Think on that!

May the truth of God's Word dawn upon our spirits—lift us above the mundane things of this life, that we may sit with Him in heavenly places, and exercise the authority that is vested in that Name, and given unto us.

Chapter 6

Authority in the Name

There is authority in the Name of Jesus. When Jesus appeared to John on the isle of Patmos, He said, *"I am he that liveth, and was dead; and, behold, I am alive for evermore . . . and have the keys of hell and of death"* (Rev. 1:18).

The one who has the key is the authorized one. Jesus is saying here, "I am the authorized one." He has authority.

Just before He ascended to be seated at the right hand of the Father, Jesus said, *"All power [authority] is given me in heaven and in earth"* (Matt. 28:18). He immediately delegated His authority in the earth to the Church, *"Go ye therefore . . . . "* (Matt. 28:19). Then He promised, *"And these signs shall follow them that believe; IN MY NAME . . . . "*

In My Name! In the Name of Jesus! He authorized us. He gave us His Name as the authority. The power is in the Name. The authority is in the Name. He gave us the Name that is above every name. He gave us the Name that is recognized in three worlds—the Name that has authority in heaven, on earth, and under the earth. Angels, men, and demons have to bow at that Name—and that Name belongs to us. We are *authorized* to use that Name.

He commissioned us: *"All authority is given me in heaven and in earth, Go ye therefore . . . And these signs shall follow them that believe; IN MY NAME shall they cast out devils; they shall speak with new tongues; They shall take up serpents; and if they drink any deadly thing, it shall not hurt them; they shall lay hands on the sick, and they shall recover"* (Matt. 28:18,19; Mark 16:17,18).

47

Some folks would tell us, "Healing has been done away with. Speaking with tongues has been done away with. The Church doesn't have any authority today over devils and demons. They can't cast them out."

No! No! No! These supernatural signs follow the Name of Jesus. They accompany the believing ones. If your spouse, or a friend, accompanies you some place, they go right along with you. These signs go right along with the believing ones.

"But that was just for the early Church," religious people tell us.

If that is so, then the Name of Jesus does not belong to us, for it is *"in my Name"* that they accompany the believing ones. If that is so, then the Name of Jesus belonged only to the early Church. And if we do not have the Name of Jesus, then no one is born again today, for there is no other Name given under heaven whereby we must be saved (Acts 4:12).

But, blessed be God, the Name of Jesus does belong to us today! And, thank God, there is salvation in that Name.

Yet there is more than salvation in that Name. That Name still enwraps all the power, all the majesty, and all the glory it ever did.

The Father God has lifted Jesus to the highest position of the universe. Jesus is seated at the right hand of the Father on high, far above every known authority. God the Father has conferred upon Him the highest Name in the universe—the Name above every name. He has bestowed upon Him honor, glory, and power.

Jesus with His resurrected body is there at the right hand of the Father. But, that Name has all the authority, all the power, all the dignity, all the majesty, and all the glory that Jesus the Person has. **The Name stands for**

the Person. This honor, this glory, this authority, this power, is vested in the Name of Jesus. And this Name is given to us!

The Church has been rich since its beginning. Yet, thinking we were being humble, we sat around and sang, "Here I wander like a beggar, through the heat and through the cold," or, "Just build me a cabin in the corner of glory land." That's not being humble. That's being ignorant. We have a rich inheritance—the Name of Jesus!

Would to God that we could catch a glimpse of what it means. Too often, the Scriptures we are studying fall on deaf ears. Would to God we would get the revelation of what God's Word says to us about it. E. W. Kenyon did. I want to quote what he has written under the subtitle, "New Land Ahead." And remember, he wrote this several years ago. We are getting more into the edge of this now than they were in the day he wrote it.

> Oh, that our eyes were open; that our souls would dare rise into the realm of Omnipotence where the Name would mean to us all that the Father has invested in it; that we would act up to our high privileges in Christ Jesus.
>
> This is practically an unexplored tableland in Christian experience.
>
> Here and there, some of us have experienced the authority vested in the Name of Jesus. We have seen the lame walk, the deaf hear, the blind see; those on the verge of death brought back instantly to health and vigor; but, so far, none of us have been able to take a permanent place in our privileges and abide where we may enjoy the fullness of this mighty power.

Smith Wigglesworth got into the edge of it. In his book, *Ever Increasing Faith*[1], he tells about going to Wales to pray for a man called Lazarus. Lazarus had been a leader

in the assembly, working in the tin mines days and
preaching nights, until he broke down physically and
collapsed. Tuberculosis set in. He lay bedfast and helpless
for six years.

God spoke to Wigglesworth and told him to go raise up
Lazarus. When Smith walked into his room, Lazarus
looked like a skeleton with skin stretched over it.
Wigglesworth endeavored to get him to release his faith;
to believe God. But he was bitter. Others had prayed for
him. He thought God should have healed him. After all, he
had given his life to Him, working days and preaching
nights.

Undaunted, Wigglesworth said to the people he was
staying with, "Could we get seven people to pray with me
for the poor man's deliverance?"

So seven people, plus Wigglesworth, went into the
room where Lazarus lay on the verge of death. The eight
believers circled the bed, holding hands. One brother took
one of Lazarus' hands; Wigglesworth took the other to
include him in the circle.

Then Wigglesworth said, "We are not going to pray; we
are just going to use the Name of Jesus." They all knelt
and whispered that one word, "Jesus! Jesus! Jesus!"

The power of God fell, and then it lifted. Five times it
fell and lifted, as the little group spoke that magnificent
Name. The man in the bed was unmoved. The sixth time
the power of God came down on that man, it remained.

"The power of God is here," Wigglesworth told him. "It
is yours to accept."

The man's lips began to move. He made a confession.
He said, "I have been bitter in my heart, and I know I have
grieved the Spirit of God. I am helpless. I cannot lift my
hands, nor even lift a spoon to my mouth."

Wigglesworth said, "Repent, and God will hear you."

He repented and cried out, "Oh God, let this be to Thy glory." When he said that, the power of God went through him.

Wigglesworth said, "As we again said, 'Jesus! Jesus! Jesus!' the bed shook, and the man shook. I said to the people who were with me, 'You can all go downstairs right away. This is all God. I'm not going to assist Him.' I sat and watched that man get up and dress himself. We sang the doxology as he walked down the steps. I said to him, 'Now tell what has happened.' It was soon noised abroad that Lazarus had been raised up and the people came from all the district round to see him and hear his testimony. And God brought salvation to many."

One of the leaders of a certain Full Gospel denomination told me of an experience he'd had in his youth. He started preaching at the age of 14. When he was 16, he held a youth meeting in Iowa and stayed in the home of the pastor, who had children near this young minister's age.

The pastor was called away to preach a funeral in another state. While he was gone, at 2 o'clock one morning, one of the church members came to the parsonage. A 3-year-old girl was very sick. She had gone into convulsions. The pastor's wife prepared to go to their home to pray. She asked the evangelist, just a 16-year-old boy, to go with her.

She was in the ministry with her husband, but she was not called to preach. So they asked the young minister to pray.

He told me, "The child was in convulsions. I laid hands on her and prayed. I did everything I had ever seen anybody do. I said everything I ever heard anybody say. Nothing happened. The child still was in convulsions.

"Then the pastor's wife began to sing, 'Praise the Lord! Glory to God! Hallelujah! Jesus! Jesus! Jesus! Jesus! Jesus! Jesus!'

"We were on our knees. One by one, we picked it up and sang praises and the Name of Jesus. While we were singing, the child suddenly grew quiet; the convulsions ceased.

"We stopped singing, sat around and visited about 10 minutes, and the child seemed fine. Then suddenly, she went back into convulsions. We prayed. I laid hands on her again, anointed her with oil, and said everything I ever heard anybody say. I rebuked the devil. I commanded the child to be well. Everything! Nothing seemed to work.

"After a little while, the pastor's wife began to sing, 'Jesus! Jesus! Jesus! Glory to Jesus! Glory to God! Jesus! Jesus!'

"One by one, we picked it up. We sang praises unto the Name, and we sang the Name. Suddenly, all convulsions ceased."

He went on with the meeting for several days. The child was perfectly well.

There is power in that Name! That is what Kenyon was talking about when he said, "Some of us have experienced the authority vested in the Name of Jesus. But, so far, none of us have been able to take a permanent place in our privileges and abide where we may enjoy the fullness of this mighty power."

Mr. Kenyon goes on to say something which expresses my convictions. I have said these very words myself.

> But we have a conviction that before the Lord Jesus returns, there will be a mighty army of believers who will learn the secret of living in the Name, of reigning in life, living the victorious, transcendant, resurrection life of the Son of God among men.

Hallelujah!

"If our minds could only grasp," Kenyon goes on, "the fact that Satan is paralyzed, stripped of his armor by the Lord Jesus, and that disease and sickness are servants of this Man; that at His voice, they must depart, it would be easy to live in this Resurrection Realm."

> **MATTHEW 8:5-10**
> 5 And when Jesus was entered into Capernaum, there came unto him a centurion, beseeching him,
> 6 And saying, Lord, my servant lieth at home sick of the palsy, grievously tormented.
> 7 And Jesus saith unto him, I will come and heal him.
> 8 The centurion answered and said, Lord, I am not worthy that thou shouldest come under my roof: but speak the word only, and my servant shall be healed.
> 9 For I am a man under authority, having soldiers under me: and I say to this man, Go, and he goeth; and to another, Come, and he cometh; and to my servant, Do this, and he doeth it.
> 10 When Jesus heard it, he marvelled, and said to them that followed, Verily I say unto you, I have not found so great faith, no, not in Israel.

What did this Roman centurion say to so marvel Jesus?

He said, in effect, "Speak the Word only. Just as I am set over these hundred men who obey my command, You have been set over disease. You are the master over demons and the laws of nature. You have authority over disease and sickness. All You have to do is speak, and sickness and disease will obey You."

---

[1] Smith Wigglesworth, *Ever Increasing Faith*, Springfield, Missouri, Gospel Publishing House.

Chapter 7

The Name:
Possession of the Church

All the authority, all the power, that was in Jesus is in
His Name! And He gave His Name to the Church. The
early believers knew what they had—and they used it.

Peter and John, going into the Temple about 3 o'clock
in the afternoon, passed by a crippled man begging alms.

ACTS 3:3-6
3 Who seeing Peter and John about to go into the
temple asked an alms.
4 And Peter, fastening his eyes upon him with John,
said, Look on us.
5 And he gave heed unto them, expecting to receive
something of them.
6 Then Peter said, Silver and gold have I none; but
SUCH AS I HAVE give I thee: IN THE NAME of Jesus
Christ of Nazareth rise up and walk.

In a later chapter, we will examine in detail the use of
the Name of Jesus in this incident, but my point here is
that Peter knew he had something.

The church world as a whole today does not know they
have anything.

Some churches do not even know they have the new
birth. They do not understand that they are new creatures.
They think all they have is forgiveness of sin.

You see, as long as I believe that I receive forgiveness
of my sins, and that's all (not remission, but just forgiveness), then I remain in the position where Satan will
dominate me all my life. But when I know I have been born
again, and have become a new man in Christ Jesus, and

that I have become the righteousness of God in Christ, then I will dominate sin (2 Cor. 5:17,21; Rom. 6:14).

Other churches are strong on the new birth; they know that you can be born again, but they do not know that you can get anything beyond that. Their attitude seems to be: "Hold out until the end, and pray that Jesus will come quickly, because the devil is taking everything over. He is bigger than God and stronger than the Church. You can just look around and see how strong he is. He is ruling and dominating everything, and he is going to take over the whole world. We're left orphans, helpless. Poor old me. I can't. I won't ever amount to anything. Pray for me that I'll hold out faithful until the end. But I don't know whether I can or not. I hope so."

That is not New Testament Christianity. That is not what the New Testament teaches.

New Testament Christianity is: *Greater is He that is in you, than he that is in the world* (1 John 4:4).

New Testament Christianity is: *I am more than a conqueror through Him that loved me* (Rom. 8:37).

New Testament Christianity is: *He hath said, I will never leave thee, nor forsake thee. So that we may boldly say, the Lord is my helper, and I will not fear what man shall do unto me* (Heb. 13:5,6).

We have defeated and robbed ourselves. Even some who knew they had the Name of Jesus did not think it amounted to much.

Charles Hadden Spurgeon (1834-92), noted English Baptist preacher, told this personal experience. He was called to the home of an elderly woman who was bedfast. Malnutrition was about to take her physical life. During his visit, Spurgeon noticed a framed document on the wall. He asked the woman, "Is this yours?"

She said it was, and explained that she had worked as a maid in the household of some of the English nobility. "Before Lady So-and-so died," the woman said, "she gave that to me. I served her for nearly half a century. I've been so proud of it because she gave it to me. I had it framed. It's been hanging on the wall ever since she died 10 years ago."

Mr. Spurgeon asked, "Would you allow me to take it and have it examined more closely?"

"Oh, yes," said the woman, who never learned to read, "just be sure to see I get it back."

Spurgeon took it to the authorities. They had been looking for it. It was a bequest. The English noblewoman had left her maid a home and money.

She lived in a little one-room house built out of wooden boxes and was starving to death—yet she had hanging on the wall a document that authorized her to be well cared for and to live in a fine house. The money was gathering interest. It belonged to her. Spurgeon helped her get it, but it didn't do her as much good as it could have earlier.

I think that is indicative of what has happened to much of the church world. We live in a little run-down shanty—spiritually speaking—while lying on a table somewhere is the New Covenant. We're proud of it. But we've never taken time to find out what it says belongs to us.

Peter knew what belonged to him when he fastened his eyes upon that life-long cripple at the Gate Beautiful and said, "*Silver and gold have I none; but SUCH AS I HAVE give I thee: IN THE NAME of Jesus Christ of Nazareth rise up and walk.*"

"You know, though," some would say, "Peter and John were apostles. The apostles had that kind of power to get the Church started. But when the last apostle died, all that ceased."

How in the world sensible men could think like that is beyond my comprehension.

The devil has hoodwinked whole denominations. He doesn't want people to find out about this Name. He's afraid of the Name. He knows Jesus conquered him. He knows that Name is just as powerful as Jesus the Person. He knows Jesus said, *"In my Name* they shall cast out devils."* (That means they will exercise authority over the devil and demons.) He knows that. He does not want you to know it. As long as you do not know it, he can continue to dominate you. So, he has hoodwinked the church world. He does not care how religious you get. As long as you don't have any power, you are no threat to him.

Then there are those who believe in the new birth, who believe in being filled with the Holy Spirit and speaking with other tongues, who believe in divine healing, who believe in the power of God—but there is confusion in this camp.

There are all kinds of ideas here. "Well, the Lord can heal *if* He wants to—but it's not always His will."

People who are filled with the Spirit, speaking with tongues, who have the Powerhouse in them, sit around and say, "Well, if we had the power, we could do what they did in the Acts of the Apostles. Pray for the power." So they sing, "Oh, Lord, send the power just now." The Power was there all the time they were singing.

The Lord could have looked over the banister of heaven and said to Gabriel, "What are they doing down there?" Gabriel might have answered, "They think they're having church, but like 2- or 3-year-old children, they're just playing church."

We have so much of that in Pentecostal and Full Gospel circles and prayer groups—playing!

No! Let's wake up and find out what belongs to us. We have had it in our hands all the time. It is ours. What is it? It is just what Peter had. *"Silver and gold have I none; but SUCH AS I HAVE give I thee . . . . "*

What did he have?

He had the Name that is above every Name.

"IN THE NAME of Jesus Christ of Nazareth rise up and walk."

He had the Name. We have the Name. The Name today is just the same.

"Well, I use the Name and nothing happens," you say. You never took time to study the Word to see what is involved in the Name; to see what is back of the Name. It is not to be used like a magic charm. It is not to be used like a rabbit's foot. You must know what is invested in that Name. You must know what is back of that Name.

You cannot say that a nice home, a good living, and money didn't belong to that poor woman Spurgeon visited. All that belonged to her. It was hers. She had the legal document, signed and sealed, which said it was hers. Why didn't she possess it? Because she didn't know it.

Thank God, we have the legal document of the New Covenant, the New Testament, sealed by the blood of Jesus Christ. And when He went away, He left us His Name. But we must know what is invested in that Name. We must know what is back of that Name.

Chapter 8

Backed by Deity

For more than a quarter of a century, a battle has raged. It started right here in America in the church world. Church groups, growing more and more "modern" ("liberal" as some call them), began to deny the deity of Jesus.

I read an article by one of the main leaders of one large denomination. In it he said, "After nearly 50 years in the ministry, I no longer believe in the virgin birth of Jesus Christ. In fact, I have come to this conclusion—you do not have to believe in the deity of Christ. I am not going to discuss it, but I will just say, I do not know whether He is the Son of God or not."

Of course, to this man, the Name of Jesus means nothing. For if Jesus is not virgin born, then He is not deity; He is not God. If He is not God, then His Name means nothing.

Kenyon said, "The deity of the Man of Galilee is the crux of Christianity. If this can be successfully challenged, then Christianity has lost its heart and it will cease to function; it will become a dead religion.

"There is no denial that the challenge of His deity has already begun its reactionary effect upon society. If Jesus is not deity, He is not Lord. If He is not Lord, then He cannot interfere with our moral activities. If He is not Lord, then the laws that have been founded upon His teachings have lost their force. The morals that surround marriage with its lofty ideals have no basis of fact."

Today we can clearly see the "reactionary effect" Kenyon talked about. We see it in our educational system. We see it in our liberal and modernistic churches. We see it in our society.

A person would have to be a fool not to see the wave of crime and lawlessness sweeping over our nation. It is a by-product of the modernist challenge to the integrity of the Lord Jesus Christ.

This battle, raged in the churches, is one reason so many people live together today without marriage. Nobody can do that and believe in the deity of the Son of God. Nobody can be permissive in sexuality and believe that Jesus Christ is deity.

If you believe He is deity, you will follow His precepts, His teachings, His morals. You will follow them in business dealings and in your daily life. For the Bible says that we must all stand—talking about Christians—before the judgment seat of Christ to give an account of the deeds done in the body (2 Cor. 5:10).

Kenyon said it so well:

> To say He was but a good man is an insult.
> To say that He was the highest expression of deity in humanity is to throw the lie into His face.
> Jesus is or He is not what He said He was.

Thanks be unto God, the Word of God is true. The Lord Jesus Christ is the Son of God. He is the Living Word. He is God manifested in the flesh. He is Truth. He is Deity. He is alive today—and He has given us His Name. *Deity* is what stands back of that Name!

Chapter 9

That Name—In Salvation

There is no salvation apart from the Name of Jesus, and apart from the Lord Jesus Christ. It is the One Name through which the sinner can approach the Great Father God.

> **MATTHEW 1:21,23**
> **21 And she shall bring forth a son, and thou shalt call his name JESUS: for he shall save his people from their sins . . . .**
> **23 Behold, a virgin shall be with child, and shall bring forth a son, and they shall call his name Emmanuel, which being interpreted is, God with us.**

> **ACTS 4:12**
> **12 Neither is there salvation in any other: for there is none other name under heaven given among men, whereby we must be saved.**

No one can get to God in any other way than by the Name of Jesus. You cannot get to God through nature. You can know that there is a God by observing nature. But you cannot get to Him through nature. You cannot come to Him in any other way than by the Name of Jesus.

"That is narrow," some people say.

If it is narrow, then it is narrow. That is what the Bible teaches. There is *"none other name"* that gives man a hearing before God's throne.

Jesus said, *"I am the way, the truth, and the life: no man cometh unto the Father, but by me"* (John 14:6).

He is *the* way. There is no other way to the Father. There is no other way to salvation. There is no other way to heaven. There is no other way to truth. There is no other way to God. There is no other way to Eternal Life—except through Jesus, and through His Name!

Chapter 10

The Name and Baptisms

The believer is not only saved by the Name—but the believer is baptized into the Name—and on the ground of the Name he receives the gift of the Holy Spirit.

MATTHEW 28:19
19 Go ye therefore, and teach all nations, baptizing them in [INTO] THE NAME of the Father, and of the Son, and of the Holy Ghost.

ACTS 2:38
38 Then Peter said unto them, Repent, and be baptized every one of you IN THE NAME OF JESUS CHRIST for the remission of sins, and ye shall receive the gift of the Holy Ghost.

The Bible teaches that there are three baptisms available to every person in the Name of Jesus: (1) baptism into the Body of Christ at the new birth; (2) baptism into water; (3) baptism into the Holy Spirit.

The fundamental principles of the doctrine of Christ are listed in Hebrews chapter 6. One is called, *"the doctrine of baptisms"* (v. 2). Note that the word "baptisms" is plural.

Someone who has not studied the Bible very deeply, but just skimmed along on the surface, might ask, "How can that be, when the Book of Ephesians says there is just one baptism?"

Paul wrote both Letters—Ephesians and Hebrews. The Spirit of God, speaking through the Apostle Paul, is talking about the entire doctrine of baptisms in Hebrews.

In Ephesians, He is talking about the one baptism that saves a person—the only baptism which puts one into the Body of Christ.

EPHESIANS 4:4,5
4 There is one body, and one Spirit, even as ye are called in one hope of your calling;
5 One Lord, one faith, one baptism . . . .

Baptism into the Body

To baptize means to immerse, to put into. When someone is born again, he is baptized into, put into, immersed into the Body of Christ.

1 CORINTHIANS 12:13
13 For by one Spirit are we all baptized into one body . . . .

Jesus is the Head. We are the Body. The Head and the Body are one. A person's head doesn't go by one name, and his body by another. People wouldn't call a man's head, James, and his body, Henry. Christ is the Head—we are the Body—and the Body of Christ is Christ. He that is joined to the Lord is one Spirit. We are one with Him.

GALATIANS 3:27,28
27 For as many of you as have been baptized into Christ have put on Christ.
28 There is neither Jew nor Greek, there is neither bond nor free, there is neither male nor female: for ye are all one in Christ Jesus.

Water Baptism

The believer can be baptized in water as an outward evidence of what has happened in the new birth.

Water baptism does not save you.

I know. I was baptized in water and I died and went to hell! I cried out in the darkness as I went down under the earth, "God! I belong to the church! I have been baptized in water!"

I was trying to tell Him He was making a mistake—I ought not to be going in that direction.

I cried louder, "God!! I belong to the church!! I've been baptized in water!!" There was no answer—only my own voice echoing through the darkness.

The third time, I literally screamed, "God!!! God!!! I belong to the church!!! I've been baptized in water!!!" There was no answer.

I came to the bottom of the pit—to the entrance of hell. Heat beat me in the face. A creature met me and took me by the right arm to escort me in.

Then a Voice spoke from heaven. It sounded like a man's voice. I do not know what He said; it was not in English. But whatever He said, thank God, it got the job done. That place shook like there was an earthquake. That creature took his hand off my arm. A suction to my back, an irresistible pull, drew me away from the gates of hell. I began to come up, head first, out of the pit. I could feel the cool breezes of the earth before I got to the top of the pit.

As I was coming up, I started praying. I said, "Father, I come to You in the Name of Jesus Christ. I repent of my sins. I ask You to forgive me."

I came up at the foot of the bed, in the south bedroom of 405 North College Street, in the city of McKinney, Texas,

April 22, 1933. I leaped from the foot of the bed, through my mouth, into my body. When I got inside my body, my physical voice picked up that prayer right where I was praying. I prayed so loudly, they tell me traffic stopped for several blocks. Thanks be unto God, I was saved!

That very moment I had peace. That very moment it was as though a two-ton weight rolled off my chest. That very moment I was born again, baptized into the Body of Christ.

Several years passed before I was baptized in water. In fact, I had been preaching and laying hands on the sick for two or three years before I was baptized in water. I knew that the first time I was baptized in water I was unsaved. I think the fellow who baptized me was probably unsaved. So I waited until I found someone who was saved and had the power of God in his life to baptize me.

Some people have gotten into controversy trying to be technical about a water baptismal formula. Baptismal formula is not going to save you.

I believe in being baptized in the Name of Jesus. I do not believe in being baptized in the name of "Jesus only."

When I baptize people in water, I say this, "In the Name of the Lord Jesus Christ, I now baptize you in the Name of the Father, and of the Son, and of the Holy Ghost."

Thank God for water baptism.

Baptism in the Holy Spirit

The believer can be baptized in the Holy Spirit, and speak with other tongues as the Spirit of God gives utterance.

Jesus said, *"For John truly baptized with water; but ye shall be baptized with the Holy Ghost not many days hence"* (Acts 1:5).

This was fulfilled on the day of Pentecost, *"And they were all filled with the Holy Ghost, and began to speak with other tongues, as the Spirit gave them utterance"* (Acts 2:4).

It is on the ground of the Name of Jesus that we receive the gift of the Holy Ghost. Peter, preaching on the day of Pentecost, said, *"Repent, and be baptized every one of you IN THE NAME of Jesus Christ for the remission of sins, and ye shall receive the gift of the Holy Ghost"* (Acts 2:38).

Jesus Himself declared, *"IN MY NAME . . . they shall speak with new tongues"* (Mark 16:17).

All in the Name

Three baptisms are available to each of us—but it is all in the Name of Jesus. Outside that Name, not one is available.

Chapter 11

The Name of Jesus
in our Daily Walk

The Name of Jesus touched every part of the early believers' lives. The Name of Jesus filled a place in their thoughts, in their prayers, in their preaching that we are almost ignorant of today. Yet in our Christian walk, in our Christian life, in prayer, we have the same right to the use of the Name of Jesus. May the Lord open our eyes and our hearts that we may know the riches of the glory of God which are hidden in that Name as we take special notice of its place in the believer's daily walk.

In Prayer

Most Christians know, to some extent, that they can use His Name in prayer—but they do not realize the significance of it.

Some repeat it in parrot-like fashion—and it does not work.

Most do not expect it to work.

Many times people have come to me, quoting Scripture, such as Matthew 18:19,20. They say, "Brother Hagin, will you agree with me about this?"

I agree with them, have a word of prayer, and then ask, "Do you agree?"

They say, "Yes, yes I do."

I say, "It's done then, isn't it?"

"Yes, it is done," they say, as they go their way.

In the process of time, in conversation with these same people, I ask them about it. They say, "Well, Brother

Hagin, I didn't much expect it to happen anyhow."

There was no agreement. I did expect it to happen.

They had quoted Jesus' promise regarding the use of His Name in the prayer of agreement—but they'd said it out of their head. It did not work because they did not agree from their heart; from their spirit. They were not in the spiritual realm. They were not in the biblical realm. They were in the natural, human realm—in the mental realm.

It is possible to repeat Scriptures, or the Name of Jesus from memory, or rote, just because somebody else says it—and it will not work.

But, blessed be God, when you know it and realize what the Word of God actually says—when you believe it from your heart—when you act on it from your heart—then it will work!

And when you actually believe God's Word from your heart, you will stay with that Word—speaking naturally now—live or die, sink or swim, go over or under. It may look sometimes as if you are going to do all of it—die, sink, go under. But as you stay with it—God will stay with His Word. It will work!

Briefly, we will look again at the classic promise Jesus made regarding the use of His Name in prayer.

> **JOHN 16:23,24**
> 23 And in that day ye shall ask me nothing. Verily, verily, I say unto you, Whatsoever ye shall ASK THE FATHER IN MY NAME, he will give it you.
> 24 Hitherto have ye asked nothing IN MY NAME: ask, and ye shall receive, that your joy may be full.

I have a key that unlocks the door of my automobile. I may say that I unlock the door, but really it is the key that does it. I have a key that fits the ignition. I couldn't start the car without that key. The key is the important factor in driving that car. I could get nowhere without it.

There is a key to prayer without which we can get nowhere. This key will unlock the doors and windows of heaven and grant our every need. This key is the Name of Jesus.

Jesus is our Mediator, Intercessor, Advocate, and Lord. He stands between us and the Father. No place in the Bible are we told to pray to Jesus. We are always told to pray to the Father in Jesus' Name. Therefore, to be sure our prayers reach the Father, we must come according to the rules laid down in the Word.

When Jesus said, "in that day," He was talking about the day we live in now. He made this promise just before He went to Calvary. The New Covenant was about to come into being. A good way to think of it is, "In the day of the New Covenant, ye shall ask Me nothing. Whatsoever ye shall ask the Father in My Name, He will give it you."

While Jesus was on the earth, His disciples did not use His Name in prayer. Hence, He said, "*Hitherto* [or up till now] *have ye asked nothing in My Name* . . . . " It was after He arose from the dead, conquered the hosts of hell, and was seated at the Father's right hand, far above all principality, power, might, and dominion, that the Church could pray in the more excellent Name He obtained—the Name above every name!

"*Ask, and ye shall receive, that your joy may be full.*" His Name guarantees an answer to our prayer!

In Demanding Our Rights

Closely associated with the Scripture we just

examined—because the Name of Jesus is involved—yet different in application is another promise Jesus made regarding the use of His Name.

> **JOHN 14:13,14**
> **13 And whatsoever ye shall ask IN MY NAME, that will I do, that the Father may be glorified in the Son.**
> **14 If ye shall ask any thing IN MY NAME, I will do it.**

Jesus is not talking about prayer here. (He is talking about prayer in John 16, because He said, "*Whatsoever ye shall ASK THE FATHER in My Name, HE WILL GIVE IT YOU.*") Here He said, "*Whatsoever ye shall ask in my name, THAT WILL I DO . . . If ye shall ask any thing in my Name, I WILL DO IT.*"

He is not talking about praying to the Father to do something. He is talking about using the Name of Jesus against the enemy in our daily life.

The word "ask" also means "demand." "Whatever you demand in My Name, I [Jesus] will do it."

An example of this is recorded in the 3rd chapter of Acts with Peter and John at the gate called Beautiful. We have already discussed that Peter knew he had something to give when he said to the crippled man, "Silver and gold have I none, but what I have I give thee . . . . "

Then Peter said, "In the Name of Jesus Christ of Nazareth, rise up and walk." He asked, or demanded, that the man get up and walk in the Name of Jesus.

I was teaching this once and a professor of Greek, who was qualified to teach the language in any university, was following along in his Greek Testament. He came to me after the service, saying, "Brother Hagin, I never thought of that until you brought it out, but the Greek literally says, 'Whatever ye shall demand as your rights and privileges, that shall I do.' " Hallelujah!

Strong's concordance brings out this meaning of the Greek word translated ask: "to demand something due."[1]

You cannot demand rights and privileges, however, if you do not know what they are. That's where Christians fail. They do not realize that under the New Covenant which God has established with the Church through the Lord Jesus Christ, we have rights and privileges.

We have the right—we have the privilege—to use the Name of Jesus! And vested in that Name is all the power, all the authority, that Jesus ever had.

When Jesus was on the earth, He healed the sick.

Now do you see what Peter did? Peter was bold. He understood what Jesus meant when He said, "Whatever you demand in My Name, I will do." So he said, "I have that Name—and it is my right to use it. So, in the Name of Jesus Christ of Nazareth, rise up and walk!"

He demanded it in Jesus' Name! And Jesus got the fellow up and put him to walking!

Read through the Book of Acts. You will see the early believers using the Name in just this way. Very little is said about their praying for the sick. They did on occasion—Paul did on the island of Melita (Acts 28:8)—but most of the time they simply used the Name of Jesus.

Several years after the healing of the man at the Gate Beautiful, for instance, Peter said to a man who had been bedfast eight years, *"Aeneas, Jesus Christ maketh thee whole: arise, and make thy bed"* (Acts 9:34). He arose immediately!

They did not have some unknown power we don't have today. It was the Name of Jesus that did it. That Name has not been taken away from the Church. That Name belongs to us.

Why doesn't that Name do now what it did then? Why doesn't that Name perform the same miracles it did then?

I think we can locate the problem from Peter's remarks to the crowd that gathered after they saw the man who had lain so many years, begging alms at the Gate Beautiful, now walking and leaping and praising God.

> **ACTS 3:12,13,16**
> 12 . . . why look ye so earnestly on us, as though by our own power or holiness we had made this man to walk?
> 13 The God of Abraham, and of Isaac, and of Jacob, the God of our fathers, hath glorified his Son Jesus; . . . .
> 16 And his name THROUGH FAITH IN HIS NAME hath made this man strong . . . .

We have had the Name, but our faith in the Name has been weak. Our faith in the Name has not been the same.

What can we do to correct this? The Bible says, *"So then faith cometh by hearing, and hearing by the word of God"* (Rom. 10:17). How can our faith in the Name of Jesus be increased? By hearing what the Word of God has to say about the Name.

We need to feed on God's Word along this line until our spirits are thoroughly educated, and our faith rises to a higher level. Then it will be just as natural for us to act on that Word as it was for Peter.

---

[1] James Strong, *Strong's Exhaustive Concordance*, Greek Dictionary of the New Testament, p. 63 (4441 comp reference to 154).

Chapter 12

All in the Name

*And whatsoever ye do in word or deed, DO ALL
IN THE NAME OF THE LORD JESUS, giving
thanks to God and the Father by him.*
                                    —Colossians 3:17

The Holy Spirit, through the Apostle Paul, gave these
instructions to the Church. Whatever you do—in word or
deed—do all in the Name of the Lord Jesus.

If you sweep the floor, sweep it in the Name of Jesus.

If you wash the dishes, wash them in the Name of
Jesus.

If you make the beds, make them in the Name of Jesus.

If you teach a Sunday School class, teach it in the Name
of Jesus.

If you sing a song, sing it in the Name of Jesus.

If you play an instrument, play it in the Name of Jesus.

If you work in a service station, work there in the
Name of Jesus.

If you work in a factory, work in the Name of Jesus.

Whatever you do! In word or in deed! Do it in the
Name! That Name has something to do with us in
everyday life. *Every* day! *Every* day, the Name!

In the early days of the Church they were taught to do
all things in that Name. Everything they did, they did it in
the Name of the Lord Jesus. Everywhere they went, they
were conscious of the Name of Jesus.

No wonder the people outside the Church feared that
Name more than anything else. The authorities who took
Peter and John into custody after the healing of the man at
the Gate Beautiful threatened them, *"that they speak*

77

*henceforth to no man IN THIS NAME. And they called
them, and commanded them not to speak at all nor teach IN
THE NAME of Jesus"* (Acts 4:17,18).

That Name should be so in our lips, and mean so much
to us, that people outside the Church today would notice.
Those authorities took notice of Peter and John, and
marvelled. Though they perceived that Peter and John
were unlearned and ignorant men, they took knowledge of
them, that they had been with Jesus (Acts 4:13).

They didn't have one Church in the first century, while
we have another Church today. We are members of the
same Body of Christ. What the Spirit of God, through the
Apostle Paul, wrote to the Church at Colosse, belongs to
the Church today. It belongs to the believers everywhere.
"Whatever you do," we are instructed, *"in word or deed, do
all in the Name of the Lord."*

Give Thanks in the Name

EPHESIANS 5:20
**20 Giving thanks always for all things unto God and
the Father IN THE NAME of our Lord Jesus Christ.**

The early believers were taught to give thanks unto
God for all His benefits *in that Name.*

Washed, Sanctified, Justified
in That Name

1 CORINTHIANS 6:11
**11 And such were some of you: but ye are washed, but
ye are sanctified, but ye are justified IN THE NAME of
the Lord Jesus, and by the Spirit of our God.**

"And such were some of you . . . . " We'd better read the

preceding verses to find out how some of us were. We will start with verse 9.

"Know ye not that the unrighteous shall not inherit the kingdom of God? Be not deceived . . . [Many people are being deceived today.] . . . *neither fornicators, nor idolaters, nor adulterers, nor effeminate* . . . [Effeminate means men who are homosexuals.] . . . *nor abusers of themselves with mankind* . . . [This means homosexuals, too, including lesbians. Don't they have any rights? Certainly, they have the right to go to hell if they want to. Every sinner has the right to reject Jesus if he wants to. But they also have the right to go to heaven. I have the right to try to keep them out of hell. The way to do it is to get the Bible to them. Jesus loved them and died for them, and we want to help them. But you do not help people by siding in with their wrongdoings. Morals are involved here, and the Bible is plain on the subject.] . . . *nor thieves, nor covetous, nor drunkards, nor revilers, nor extortioners, shall inherit the kingdom of God"* (1 Cor. 6:9,10).

My! That is a terrible catalog of sins.

But, praise God for the power in the Name of Jesus. The next verse says, *"And such were some of you: but you are washed, but you are sanctified, but you are justified IN THE NAME of the Lord Jesus Christ! . . . . "*

Giving Thanks to His Name

HEBREWS 13:15
15 By him therefore let us offer the sacrifice of praise to God continually, that is, the fruit of our lips giving thanks TO HIS NAME.

Continually! We are to do this continually! We are to offer the sacrifice of praise continually—that is, the fruit of our lips giving thanks to His Name.

Anointing in the Name

JAMES 5:14
14 Is any sick among you? let him call for the elders of the church; and let them pray over him, anointing him with oil IN THE NAME OF THE LORD . . . .

There it is again. Everything the early believers did, they did in the Name. They anointed the sick *in the Name of the Lord.*

Believe on the Name

1 JOHN 3:23
23 And this is his commandment, That we should BELIEVE ON THE NAME of his Son Jesus Christ, and love one another, as he gave us commandment.

We are not only told to believe on the Lord Jesus Christ—but we are told to believe on the Name. The New Covenant commandment is that we love one another, and believe in the Name.

Chapter 13

In My Name Cast Out Demons

The very first sign Jesus said would follow the believing ones is, *"In my name shall they cast out devils"* (Mark 16:17). In other words, they shall exercise authority over demons.

He did not say that this sign would follow preachers. It is not just ministers who have authority over demons in the Name of Jesus, but all believers.

Believers should *know* that they have this authority.

The Bible, our textbook, records the following example. In the Name of Jesus, Paul cast a demon out of a possessed girl, set her free, and stirred the city of Ephesus to its very foundation.

> **ACTS 16:16-18**
> 16 And it came to pass, as we went to prayer, a certain damsel possessed with a spirit of divination met us, which brought her masters much gain by sooth-saying:
> 17 The same followed Paul and us, and cried, saying, These men are servants of the most high God, which shew unto us the way of salvation.
> 18 And this did she many days. But Paul, being grieved, turned and said to the spirit, I command thee IN THE NAME OF JESUS CHRIST to come out of her. And he came out the same hour.

Notice that this damsel was "possessed with a spirit." Paul did not speak to the girl. He spoke to the spirit. He said to the spirit, *"I command thee in the name of Jesus*

Christ to come out of her. And he came out the same hour"
(v. 18).

That spirit had to come out. No possibility existed of its
not doing so. Remember that Philippians 2:9,10 says,
*"Wherefore God also hath highly exalted him, and given
him a name which is above every name: that at the name of
Jesus every knee should bow, of things [beings] in heaven,
and things [beings] in earth, and things [beings] under the
earth."*

That spirit had to bow to the Name. Demons have to go
at that Name. It is the Name that does it. And that Name
has for the Church today the same power it had then. What
a treasure we have in the Name of Jesus—and yet, how we
have neglected it.

E. W. Kenyon remarked:

> One would naturally think in reading our modern
> religious literature, and listening to the average preacher's
> sermons, that demons had gone out of existence, or else they
> had been herded together in the slums of the city and were
> spending their entire time among the lower strata of
> humanity.

In December 1952, as a pastor and I were praying in
the kitchen of his parsonage, the Lord Jesus Christ
appeared to me in a vision. He said, "I am going to teach
you concerning the devil, demons, and evil spirits. For
from this night forward what is known in my Word as
'discerning of spirits' will operate in your life and ministry
when you are in the spirit."

I was caught up in that vision for an hour and a half as
Jesus taught me.

During the vision, I saw a spirit operating through a
certain individual, harrassing a pastor and creating

problems which could have caused a split in the church.

"Do not deal with the person," Jesus said to me. "Deal with the spirit."

(We have missed it by trying to deal with the person. Paul spoke to the spirit; not to the damsel.)

"How do I do that?" I asked. The pastor was in the same state I was in, but that person was in another part of the country.

"There is no distance in the realm of the spirit," the Lord said. "Simply speak to that spirit and command him, in my Name, saying, 'You foul spirit that is operating in the life of (He called the person's name), that is harrassing and embarrassing the ministry of the servant of the Lord (calling his name), I command you to desist in your operation and stop in your maneuvers this moment.' "

In the vision, I could see the spirit which was operating through that individual. When I said what Jesus told me to say, that spirit cowered down, whimpering and whining like a whipped puppy.

Then he spoke to me, "I know I have to go if you tell me to, but I sure don't want to."

I said, "I told you, in the Name of Jesus Christ."

It was not so much that he was afraid of me—Kenneth Hagin—per se, but he remembered how Jesus died and went to hell in my place, and how, down in the dark regions of the damned, in Satan's own kingdom, Jesus defeated him. He remembered how Jesus rose up and hurled back the forces of darkness; how He spoiled principalities and powers. He remembered how Jesus paralyzed Satan. He remembered how He dethroned him. So that spirit was afraid. At the Name of Jesus, he left, and never caused that man's ministry any more trouble.

A short time later, I was holding a meeting in Pueblo,

Colorado. A man came up in the line while we were laying hands on the sick. He told me he was nervous, and couldn't sleep. (His wife told me later he'd had mental problems and had been unable to work for six months. Doctors had told her that sending him to the state mental institution was the next necessary step.)

I laid hands on him and prayed for his healing—that his nerves would be healed, and that he would be able to sleep. Then I went on to pray for the next person in the line. I continued ministering to four or five more individuals. About ten minutes had gone by since this man had gone back to his seat, which was on my right.

I happened to glance over his way—and with my eyes wide open, God allowed me to see into the spirit realm. (The gift of discerning of spirits is seeing or hearing into the spirit realm.) I saw, sitting on his right shoulder, a demon. It looked like a little monkey. It had an arm lock around his head. I understood what was wrong with the man.

I said to him, "Come back up here."

As he walked up, I could see the demon sitting on his shoulder as plainly as I could see the man.

I said to the demon, "You're going to have to leave."

He said, "I know it. I know I do, if you tell me to."

I said, "In the Name, in the Name of the Lord Jesus Christ, you leave this man's mind and body now." I saw him fall off the man's shoulder, down to the floor. He lay there whimpering, and whining, and shaking. I said, "Not only leave his body, but leave these premises." He ran out a side door.

The man lifted his hands and began to praise God. His face lit up. Then he said, and he did not know until I told him afterwards what I had seen, "It seemed like there was an iron band around my head, and it just snapped. I'm free! I'm free!" I saw him 16 years later, and he was still free.

When the Lord has permitted me to see into the spirit realm, every single time those spirits would tremble and jerk. But that always happens whether I see it or not, because I know the authority of Jesus' Name. And I can talk to the devil without seeing him—just as I can talk to God without seeing Him.

If this truth ever dawns on our hearts as believers, then life will be different: *That Name belongs to us, and the devil is frightened of us.*

A certain church I held a meeting in was the most difficult church to preach in I have ever seen. The people were good people. They loved the Lord. They loved my preaching. But it was tough to preach there. The very atmosphere was hard. Everything I said seemed to bounce off the wall back into my face.

Some months later I was back in the area, preaching a revival at another church. I went back to this first church and spent some time with the pastor and his family. I spoke at a New Year's Eve watch night service for them. The next day, the pastor's wife asked, "Brother Hagin, can you see any difference in our church?"

I said, "What do you mean?"

She said, "Is it any easier to preach? What about the pulpit now?"

I said, "There's as much difference as between daylight and dark. It doesn't seem like the same pulpit. It doesn't seem like the same church."

She said, "Get my husband to tell you about it."

He said, "I don't tell people about it, because they might think I am crazy."

(The spiritual world ought to be as real to us as water is

to a fish—because that is the world we're swimming around in. Yet when someone touches that spiritual world occasionally, since most of the church lives in the natural and is motivated by the flesh, they think that person is crazy, a fanatic.)

"I won't tell everybody," the pastor said, "but I will tell you. I got so concerned. This was the hardest church I ever preached in. The pulpit seemed to hold me in bondage. I knew the people loved me. They supported us well. We had good fellowship with them in their homes. But that pulpit was like a prison.

"I began to fast and pray about it. The seventh day of my fast, I was kneeling on the platform about three feet behind the pulpit, when I happened to look up directly over the pulpit. The ceiling disappeared."

Discerning of spirits came into manifestation. God allowed him to see into the spirit realm. He saw, sitting up in the rafters directly above the pulpit, a huge spirit. It looked like a big baboon. It was as large as a man.

The pastor said, "I found myself saying to him, 'You're going to have to come down.' He said nothing, but he seemed to draw up as if he didn't want to obey. I said, 'You come down in the Name of the Lord Jesus Christ.'

"He fell down onto the pulpit; then jumped to the floor. I said to him, 'You get out of here!' He said nothing, but looked at me as if to say, 'I don't want to.' I said, 'Just march right out of here, in the Name of Jesus.' He marched down off the platform. I marched right behind him. He would go four or five steps; then stop and look at me, almost begging. I would say, 'No, go on.' But he wouldn't move until I said, 'In the Name of Jesus.'

"We went down the aisle that way, stopping every four or five steps. I went ahead of him and held the vestibule doors open. (The spirit could have gone through the doors, of course, but this is what the pastor did.) That thing would not go through until I said, 'In the Name of Jesus.'

"Then I opened the front door. I stepped back and said, 'Move on out.' He stood there. He never said a word, but I could tell by the expression on his face, he was begging me, 'Don't!' I said, 'In the Name of Jesus,' and he moved.

"He went down the church steps and got half way out into the yard. Then he stopped, turned around, and looked at me again. I said, 'No, you don't. You go on in the Name of Jesus.'

"He went as far as the curb. I said, 'You'll have to go on. And don't ever come on these premises again.' He stood there until I said, 'In the Name of Jesus.' Then he ran across the street and down the other side about a quarter of a mile. I watched him run into a nightclub called The Green Hut. The next night it burned.

"Ever since, it is easy to preach here. The people have noticed. They have asked, 'What happened?' But I didn't tell them."

After Jesus appeared to me in 1952 and taught me from the Word of God on the subject of demons, I was led to study this subject in more detail. I found that the Scriptures teach a great deal about demons, their habits, their influence, their power over men.

Ephesians 6 points out a combat. This combat is not with fellow human beings; it is not with flesh and blood.

EPHESIANS 6:12
12 For we wrestle not against flesh and blood, but against principalities, against powers, against the rulers of the darkness of this world, against spiritual wickedness in high places.

Read the entire passage (Ephesians 6:11-18) and you will find that this combat is particularly tied to the area of prayer.

Listen to what Paul wrote to the Church at Colosse concerning a minister named Epaphras.

COLOSSIANS 4:12
12 Epaphras, who is one of you, a servant [minister] of Christ, saluteth you, always labouring [striving] fervently for you in prayers, that ye may stand perfect and complete in all the will of God.

The Greek word translated *labouring* in the King James is rendered by other translations as *striving*. It means to wrestle, to struggle, to combat. Epaphras was always wrestling, struggling, combating for the Colossians in his prayers.

With whom was he struggling? With whom was he agonizing? Certainly not with God the Father. It is God's will to bless men.

Prayer does not change God. God does not change. There is not even a shadow of turning with Him (James 1:17).

We can pray according to God's will (the Bible) and receive the provisions He has made for us. But we do not strive, wrestle, struggle, and combat with Him. The wrestling is with the unseen force that is intelligently warring against the purpose of God.

That unseen force, of course, is the devil, and demons and all their activity. He wars against God's plan.

He has warred against the ministry God called me to fulfill. I would shut myself up in the last church I pastored for two and three days at a time—just fasting and praying. God was dealing with me about leaving the pastorate and going out into field ministry. So, I left that church in 1949 and went out on the field. I've been there ever since.

But I'll tell you, those first six months, I fought more demons than I had in fifteen years of ministry put together. They ganged up on me. You see, if they could have thwarted God's plan, they would have stopped what we are doing today. There was a struggle! And I didn't know everything I know now. (That's how I learned a lot of things.)

Demons dominate people in more ways than we realize, too. They try to stop people from coming to God. They try to hold Christians back from spiritual development.

In October 1963, I came to Tulsa to speak on a Saturday night at a Full Gospel Business Men's banquet, and then to teach the following Monday through Friday, a Holy Spirit seminar for the FGBMFI. We held the seminar in a local church. God began to move—and instead of five nights, the meeting lasted eight weeks.

I ministered in two services a day—morning and night—for those eight weeks. One afternoon, between services, I was in one of the Sunday School rooms praying about the night service. I had grown tired on my knees, and was lying flat on my back on the carpet, praying in other tongues.

Suddenly, the Spirit of God spoke to me about my son-in-law, Buddy Harrison.

Reverend Harrison is at this writing founding pastor of Faith Christian Fellowship in Tulsa, Oklahoma. He is also president of Harrison House Publishers. But in 1963, he had problems.

He was unable to stay with anything. He would not keep a job; he'd just quit and and walk off. He wouldn't stay in church. One time we'd see him, and he'd be in church, leading the choir, and everything would be fine. The next time we'd see him, he would be out of church, and he would walk up to me and blow cigar smoke in my face. I never said anything. I just loved him. I knew the devil had hold of him. He was a roller-coaster, or a yo-yo Christian. Up and down. In and out.

So, while I was lying there flat on my back, praying in other tongues about the night's service, suddenly the Spirit of God said to me, "There are three demons that follow Buddy around."

I had a quick spiritual vision. I saw him walking down the sidewalk. What looked like three little dogs were following him—one on the right edge of the sidewalk, one on the left edge, and one in the middle.

The Spirit of God said, "He will turn to the right and yield to the demon on the right. Then he will turn and yield to the demon on the left. Then he will turn and yield to the demon in the center. It seems at times that he is almost a different person."

Whatever the demon was that he yielded to, Buddy would act that way. Relatives had even remarked, "I don't understand Buddy. Is he schizophrenic?"

Buddy was a born-again, Spirit-filled Christian. But just because you are filled with the Holy Spirit does not mean you are incapable of yielding to the devil. You still have a will of your own. You can yield to the devil and let the devil dominate you anytime you want. You can yield to the flesh, and let the flesh dominate you. You can yield to the world, and let the world dominate you. The Bible teaches that we have to deal with the world, the flesh, and the devil. But you do not have to yield to any of these, thank God.

The Lord said to me, "You speak to those spirits. Command them in my Name, the Name of Jesus, to desist in their maneuvers. Command them to stop."

I said, "I'm in Oklahoma. Buddy is in Texas."

He said, "In the spirit realm there is no distance."

I said, "Tell me again just how I do that."

He said, "You say, 'In the Name of the Lord Jesus Christ, I command all three of you foul spirits following Buddy around, to desist in your maneuvers and stop in your operations.' "

I rose to a seated position and said that.

Then the Word of the Lord came unto me saying, "Within ten days he will have a job. He will stay with that job until he does something else I have for him."

I wrote it down on a piece of paper, dated it, and put it in my billfold. The next time I saw Buddy, he said, "Dad, I got a job." I said, "I know it." I pulled that piece of paper out and handed it to him. He said, "That's the very day I got the job," as he counted ten days from the day it was dated.

He stayed with that job and made a success of it. They made him assistant manager—and wanted to make him manager of another business. But God called him to Minneapolis to be a choir director in a church.

His boss told someone who told me what he said, "I don't undersand that young man. He went off up there to be a song leader for $100 a week. I offered him $20,000 a year to manage this business. I guaranteed him $30,000 within 18 months. There is no doubt that in 5 years he could be making $50,000 or $60,000."

But he wanted to obey God—and he's been going with God ever since.

I did not wrestle with flesh and blood. I did not deal with Buddy. Our problem is that we keep dealing with the person—when the problem may not be with the person.

As a pastor, I saw people who seemed to be held by unseen forces. This caused me great concern. I wondered how I could help them. Many times, I was led to command the unseen powers broken over them. It worked. I just said, "In the Name of Jesus, I command Satan's power broken over this life." Instantly, the person was delivered. I've seen that happen over and over again.

Here is what Kenyon said along this line:

> I found that the reason many men did not accept Jesus as their Saviour was because they were held by the power of demons.
>
> The people are hungry; they want deliverance from sin; they crave eternal life, but they are unable, many of them, to break loose from the bonds that are holding them.
>
> Hundreds of people have said to me, "I cannot become a Christian. I want to, but something holds me."
>
> I have simply laid my hand on their shoulder and said, "In the Name of Jesus of Nazareth, I command the power that holds you, broken. Now, in His mighty Name, get on your feet."
>
> With tears of joy, they have obeyed.
>
> I have prayed with men who were held by habits— tobacco, liquor, lusts, and, in the same mighty Name, I have seen them delivered, usually instantaneously.

I do not believe God wants His children bound by anything. I just refuse to let anything dominate me.

As a young Baptist pastor of a little country church, I took a job in a store at Christmas time to have some extra money. Several times a day, we clerks would take turns buying cola-type soft drinks from the restaurant next door. I was drinking four to six a day. When the job was over, every time I went by that cafe, I just had to have a cola. One day, I stopped still in front of that cafe, and said,

"I will not let colas dominate me. From this day forward, I will never drink another one." I have not had one from that day to this, and it has been nearly half a century.

I did not say it is a sin to drink colas. But if you are a colaholic, a coffeeholic, an alcoholic, or any other kind of holic, do not let it dominate you. If you just have to have something, quit it. It will affect your faith—it will keep your faith from working.

I refuse to let anything dominate me. I drink iced tea. A while back it seemed as if I couldn't get along without it. So I quit a while—just to prove I didn't have to have it.

A man came to me after a night service with tears. He said, "Brother Hagin, you haven't condemned me, but my own heart condemns me. I'm 63 years old. I've smoked cigarettes since I was 12. I want to be free. Can you help me?"

I said, "I sure can. All you have to do is give me permission to do it."

He said, "I give you permission. I want to be helped."

I laid my hand on his shoulder, and said, "In the Name of Jesus, I break the power of nicotine over your life. And I am going to say this by faith: the next cigarette you smoke will make you sick."

He told me later, "I went home that night. Usually the last thing I did before going to bed was smoke a cigarette. I don't know why, but I didn't smoke that night. I didn't smoke the next morning. I did put the cigarettes in my pocket as I left the house."

This man was a truck driver. He picked up a fellow he knew that morning. The passenger was smoking when he got in the truck.

"I never got so sick in my life," the man told me. "I rolled down the window to get some air. Finally, I had to ask him to put out his cigarette."

This man came for help. I couldn't do that for just anyone. They may not want to be helped. But, thank God, when people want to be helped, there is authority in the Name of Jesus to help them.

Demons attempt to hinder people in every aspect of spiritual life. They try to keep people from all the blessings of God.

Christians who felt too timid to testify, or to pray in public have had their tongues loosed instantly, in the Name of Jesus.

We must always be sensitive to the Holy Spirit when dealing with people. In praying for Christians to be filled with the Spirit, for instance, sometimes it is the devil that's holding them back. It isn't always, but I am sensitive to the Holy Spirit when I pray with people, and I know when it is.

I knew that it was with one woman when she told me how many years she had been seeking. I laid my hand on her shoulder and said, "I rebuke you, foul spirit of doubt. In the Name of Jesus, leave this woman." Instantly, she started talking in tongues.

This has happened time and time again. I just lay my hands on the person's shoulder, and very calmly, very quietly, sometimes under my breath, I say, "I rebuke every devil that is holding this person." Instantly they lift both hands and start talking in tongues.

Chapter 14

Can a Christian Be Possessed?

People have muddied the water on this demon business. It is to be regretted that the Church either gets into the ditch on one side of the road or the other, instead of going down the middle.

You hear the question: Can a Christian be possessed?

Man is a spirit—he has a soul—and he lives in a body. When one is fully possessed, the devil has taken over his spirit, his soul (mind), and his body. The person would be insane. Here in the United States, because we have so much light, and so much Christianity, we seldom see a truly demon-possessed person.

My son-in-law, for instance, was not possessed of the devil. He yielded to the devil.

The mad man of Gadera, the Bible says, was "possessed" with a devil, and "had" a legion (Mark 5:15). One devil possessed him; a legion indwelt him. He was taken over completely, spirit, soul, and body.

A Christian cannot be taken over *spirit*, soul, and body. So, a Christian is not demon-possessed.

But here is another question: Can a Christian have a demon?

Decidedly, yes!

Some people are possessed with money. Money is their god—it dominates them. I have money, but I am not possessed with money.

Someone can have a demon and not be possessed. Sometimes it is in the flesh, the body.

In dealing with sickness, Jesus sometimes cast out a demon. In one case, for instance, He said, *"Thou dumb and deaf spirit, I charge thee, come out of him, and enter no more into him"* (Mark 9:25). That demon was not in the person's spirit—it was in his body.

EPHESIANS 4:27
27 Neither give place to the devil.

If a Christian knows his rights, and how to keep the devil out, he cannot come in. But if not, he can come in.

Many Christians unconsciously yield to the devil. They don't mean to—they just don't know any better.

Let's get clear on the subject. Let's not be led by fanaticism. But, let's not get over on the other side and deny their existence.

When the devil is working in some churches, they deny that the devil and demons even exist.

Corinth was a licentious city. Immoral spirits which dominated the city got into the Church. Paul wrote the Church at Corinth, saying, *"It is reported commonly that there is fornication among you . . . . "* (1 Cor. 5:1). Sure the Church was saved. Sure they were filled with the Spirit. But I'll tell you this, that's not the last church demons have gotten into.

Chapter 15

Three Necessary Steps

Three things are necessary to take deliverance and victory over demons.

First, you must be a child of God.

The seven sons of Sceva saw Paul casting out demons in the Name of Jesus. So they tried it. They found a man who was demon possessed and they said, "We adjure you by Jesus whom Paul preacheth" (Acts 19:13).

The evil spirit used the man's voice and said, "Jesus I know, and Paul I know; but who are you?" (v. 15).

Then that lone man in whom the evil spirit was, jumped on those seven fellows, overcame them, and pulled their clothes off them, so that they fled out of the house naked and wounded.

They had no right to use that Name. That Name belongs to the children of God. That Name belongs to us. To use that Name, you must be sure you are a child of God.

Second, you must not have any unconfessed, or unforgiven sin in your heart.

If you do, demons will laugh at your prayers.

The Bible says, *"Beloved, if our heart condemn us not, then have we confidence toward God"* (1 John 3:21).

You will have boldness also in the presence of demons. Don't let the devil bother you over your past life. If you've confessed it, you're forgiven (1 John 1:9). Laugh in his face.

Third, you must know the power of the Name of Jesus—and how to use it.

Jesus put them to nought! That means He reduced them to nothing. Now they are being brought to nothing by us. They are doomed to pass away eventually. But they are being brought to nothing right now, because Jesus defeated them and gave us His Name to use against them.

"In my Name, they will exercise authority over them," Jesus said. Another way to say that is, "In my Name, demons will be rendered useless. They will be brought to nothing."

When you know that, you will do as I do. When the devil attacks, I start laughing. I say, "Nothing, get on out of here." I call him "Nothing."

Some people open the door to the devil and say, "Come on in." They get up in church and brag and testify about what all he is doing.

I like the way the New English Bible says it:

> **1 CORINTHIANS 2:6,** *New English Bible*
> **6 ... not a wisdom belonging to this passing age, nor to any of its *GOVERNING POWERS, WHICH ARE DECLINING TO THEIR END.***

Declining to their end! The devil has hoodwinked the church world. People keep talking about how strong the devil is getting. The Bible says he's declining. He isn't growing stronger—especially in our lives. He's declining to the end.

Why is he holding sway in so many lives? Because they do not know the power of the Name of Jesus.

That's the reason for this book—to teach people what their rights and privileges are.

Now let's look at several translations of 1 Corinthians 2:6:

> *King James*
> **... Howbeit we speak wisdom among them that are perfect: yet not the wisdom of this world, nor of THE PRINCES OF THIS WORLD, THAT COME TO NOUGHT.**

Moffatt
... only it is not the wisdom of this world or of THE DETHRONED POWERS WHO RULE THIS WORLD.

Young's Literal Translation
... and wisdom not of this age, NOR OF THE RULERS OF THIS AGE—OF THOSE BECOMING USE-LESS ....

Amplified
... we do impart a higher wisdom; but it is indeed not a wisdom of this present age nor of this world OR OF THE LEADERS AND RULERS OF THIS AGE, WHO ARE BEING BROUGHT TO NOTHING AND ARE DOOMED TO PASS AWAY.

E. W. Kenyon wrote:

> I cannot conceive how successful work can be done today, or how believers can be in a place of continual victory, unless they know that the source of their danger lies in demoniacal power *[Don't stop there. Some people magnify the demonic powers; that is all they talk about. Kenyon did not stop there.]*, and that the power to conquer it is in the Name of Jesus of Nazareth, the Son of God.
>
> The more quickly we recognize that the very air about us is filled with hostile forces, who are attempting to destroy our fellowship with the Father, and to deprive us of our usefulness in the service of our Master, the better it will be for us.

They exist. These principalities and powers and rulers of this age, rule.

We see visible people ruling as heads of governments. Yet behind the scene, very often, wicked spirits are dominating those people.

We must keep in mind, though, that Jesus spoiled

principalities and powers. The same principalities and powers we wrestle against, He spoiled! He made a show of them openly, triumphing over them in it!

COLOSSIANS 2:15
15 And having spoiled principalities and powers, he made a shew of them openly, triumphing over them in it.

Chapter 16

Wicked Spirits
in the Heavenlies

*For we wrestle not against flesh and blood,
but against principalities, against powers,
against the rulers of the darkness of this world,
against SPIRITUAL WICKEDNESS IN HIGH
PLACES.*

—Ephesians 6:12

The margin of a good reference Bible renders that last
phrase, *"wicked spirits in the heavenlies."*

Are there wicked spirits in heaven?

Bible scholars agree that the Apostle Paul was talking
about his own experience when he said, *"I knew a man in
Christ above fourteen years ago, (whether in the body, I
cannot tell; or whether out of the body, I cannot tell: God
knoweth;) such an one caught up to the THIRD
HEAVEN ... How that he was caught up into PARA-
DISE, and heard unspeakable words . . . . "* (2 Cor. 12:2,4).

The Bible speaks of three heavens. First, the
atmospheric heaven right above us. Above that is the
heaven where the stars are. Above that is the Heaven of
heavens, Paradise, where the throne of God is.

When Ephesians 6:12 says, "wicked spirits in the
heavenlies," it is talking about the first heaven—the
atmosphere right around us.

The atmosphere around us is literally infested with
demons and evil spirits. That is the teaching of the Word of
God.

I think most Christians know the first two prerequisites (see preceding chapter), but they do not know the third step as they should. They do not know the power of the Name of Jesus—and how to use it.

The Bible is our textbook.

I've read a lot of books along this line, but I can't swallow everything in them because it is not in line with the Bible. The authors may be good people. They may be friends of mine. I may love them in the Lord, but I cannot go along with all they say because it is not in line with the Acts of the Apostles; it is not in line with the Word of God. I will not follow anybody when they get away from the Word.

The Name of Jesus will work now just like it did in the days of the Acts of the Apostles. Dealing with demons will work now just like it did then.

Read the Book of Acts carefully. Notice how the disciples used the Name. Underline, or write down, all the verses relative to how they used the Name in connection with demons. See what happened—instantly, usually.

If your own life has been defeated and hemmed in by the power of the adversary, rise up in that Almighty Name of Jesus, hurl back the enemy, and take your deliverance. Then go and set others free.

You will not be able to set others free until you get free yourself. Start dealing with the devil in your own life. I don't mean you have to cast a devil out of yourself. But the devil is arrayed against you—just like he is against me. We wrestle not against flesh and blood, but against principalities and powers. If the Church then wrestled against them, we wrestle against them now. But we shall enter into that combat with the consciousness that JESUS IS THE VICTOR!

Make these confessions aloud with your mouth
because you believe what you are saying with your heart:

> The Name of Jesus belongs to me.
> In the Name of Jesus, I have authority over demons.
> I refuse to be dominated by any demon.
> In the Name of Jesus, Satan, I break your power
>   over my spirit, soul, and body;
>   any way that you would try to dominate me.
> And I proclaim my deliverance and victory.
>
> You are a defeated foe.
> Jesus dethroned you and all of your cohorts.
> I am no longer afraid of you.
> One time, Satan, you were my master,
>   and I was your slave.
> But now I am your master;
> Because Jesus has made me master
>   over all evil powers, over all demons,
> And I am free!
> It is written,
> Whom the Son has set free, is free indeed.
> I'm free indeed!
> I'm free indeed!
>
> The Master said,
> Ye shall know the truth, and the truth shall make you
> free.
> Now I know the truth . . .
> Jesus has defeated you.
> Demons, all evil spirits, and Satan himself are subject
>   to the Name of Jesus.
> For every knee should bow,
> Of things, or beings, in heaven, in earth,
>   and under the earth.
> Heaven, earth, and hell know,
> That God raised Jesus up from the dead,
> And has seated Him at His own right hand,

Far above all principalities,
  and powers,
  and might,
  and dominion,
And has given Him a NAME!
ABOVE EVERY NAME!
And that Name belongs to me.
There's Power in that Name!
There's Glory in that Name!
There's Majesty in that Name!
There's Authority in that Name!

And I have a right to use that Name!
So, Satan, be gone!
Sickness, be gone!
Pain, leave my body!
All evil, leave me!
I stand free!
For I know the truth.
The truth has set me free!

Chapter 17

In Him

People often ask me about studying the Bible. Although I have many suggestions, there is one I present above all others.

I present it here to you. As a Christian, a believer, read through the New Testament—primarily, the Epistles, for the Epistles are the letters written to the Church.

As you read, look for all expressions such as: in Christ, in Him, in Whom, through Whom, etc. Underline them. There are approximately 140 such Scriptures which tell you *who you are, what you are,* and *what you have* because you are in Christ.

They show you your position as a believer. (You are in Christ!) They show you your legal standing. They show you your place in the family of God. They show you your place in God's purpose and plan.

By studying these Scriptures, you will find out what God's Word says about you. You will come to see your place in Christ. You will see that when Jesus gave the Church the right to use His Name, He authorized us to be His representatives in the earth.

In fact, in the Epistles, the Church is called Christ! The Church has not yet realized that we are Christ. No, we're not divine as He is, but we're joint-heirs with Him—we're His Body sent forth to work in the earth on His behalf. When we realize this, we'll start doing the work we're supposed to do.

2 CORINTHIANS 6:14-16
**14 Be ye not unequally yoked together with un-
believers: for what fellowship hath RIGHTEOUS-**

NESS with unrighteousness? and what communion hath LIGHT with darkness?

15 And what concord hath CHRIST with Belial? or what part hath HE THAT BELIEVETH with an infidel?

16 And what agreement hath THE TEMPLE OF GOD with idols? for ye are the temple of the living God; as God hath said, I will dwell in them, and walk in them; and I will be their God, and they shall be my people.

The *believer* is told not to be unequally yoked with unbelievers.

Then the believer is called *righteousness*, and the unbeliever is called unrighteousness.

The believer is called *light*; the unbeliever is called darkness (v. 14).

Now, notice the next statement. *"And what concord hath CHRIST with Belial?"* (v. 15). The believer is called Christ! We are identified with Him!

The Church is called *believers*. The Church is called *righteousness*. The Church is called *light*. The Church is called *Christ!* That's who we are! We are His representatives on the earth.

Christ is the Head; we are the Body. We are one with Christ, joined with Him in a living union. We're not gods, but we've been given the right to use Jesus' Name and to act on His behalf.

You see, that's what Jesus is saying. "Take my Name. Be my representatives."

Christ, with His resurrected flesh-and-bone body, is at the right hand of the Father. We are here as His representatives—not only collectively, but individually.

When we pray in Jesus' Name, we are taking the place
of the absent Christ; we are using His name, using His
authority to carry out His will on the earth.

—Kenyon

As He Is

Unless you are really grounded in the Scriptures, it may
not seem to you that the following Scripture could be true.
But it is:

1 JOHN 4:17
**17 Herein is our love made perfect, that we may have
boldness in the day of judgment: because AS HE IS,
SO ARE WE IN THIS WORLD.**

As who is?
As Jesus is!
So are we, where? when we get to heaven?
No! In this world! Glory!
As Jesus is, so are we in this world! And Jesus is the
same yesterday, and today, and forever (Heb. 13:8).
Jesus is the same right now as He was when He walked
the shores of Galilee.
He is the same right now as He was when blind
Bartimaeus, a beggar, sat by the wayside outside the city
of Jericho, and cried out, "Jesus! Have mercy on me!"
People around, evidently even the disciples, tried to get
him to hush. But he would not.
Jesus stopped still, and commanded him to be called.
He said unto him, "What wilt thou that I should do unto
thee?"
The blind beggar answered, "Lord, that I might receive
my sight."

In one place the Word says that Jesus had *compassion* on him.

Keep that in mind. Then consider "as He is," and, "Jesus Christ, the same yesterday, and today, and forever."

He is now all that He ever was—and as He is, so are we in this world. Jesus had compassion, and healed.

John G. Lake, mighty apostle of God, went to South Africa around the turn of the century. In five years, he built 500 churches there.

The wife of one of the government leaders was at the point of death with terminal cancer. Knowing that Lake taught divine healing, the husband asked him to come and pray.

Because of great pain, the woman was taking pain-relieving drugs. But she made the decision to stop. She said, "I'm going to throw myself completely over on the mercy of God. I'm not even going to take anything for pain."

Lake said, "If that's your stand, and that's your faith, we'll stand with you."

He and some other ministers stayed by her bedside praying 24 hours a day. The only way she could get any rest was for them to pray until she fell off to sleep.

One morning Lake went home to bathe and change clothes. On his way back, within two blocks of the house, he heard her screaming in agony. He rushed back to the house. He stated that as he ran, compassion overtook him. He rushed into the house, rushed up to the bed, and without thinking, he picked up the woman's emaciated body and held her in his arms as he sat on the bed and wept in compassion. While he was weeping, she was completely healed—every symptom of terminal cancer left.

I've noticed in my own ministry that when I can yield to the Spirit of God and allow the compassion of Jesus to well up in me and flow out of me, greater healings take place.

We have His Name.

We have His authority.

We have His compassion.

As He is, so are we in this world!

> . . . we take Jesus' place and use Jesus' Name just as though Jesus Himself were here.
>
> The only difference is that instead of Jesus doing it, we are doing it for Him; we are doing it at His command.
>
> He has given to us the same authority He had when He was here, and the believer's position in Christ gives him the same Standing with the Father that Christ had when He was here.
>
> —Kenyon

Let that soak through to your inner consciousness. It's an absolute Bible fact. We have the same standing with God that Christ had when He was here on earth.

Jesus was praying for believers—and we are included—in the 17th chapter of John. In His prayer He said:

JOHN 17:23
23 I in them, and thou in me, that they may be made perfect in one; and that the world may know that thou hast sent me, and HAST LOVED THEM, AS THOU HAST LOVED ME.

What did Jesus say? He said that the Father loved them, the believers, *as he loves Jesus*. He doesn't love Jesus any more than He loves us!

An outstanding Bible scholar said, "I wish I could believe that."

Thank God, I can. I can believe it because it is in the Word. He loves us the same. We have the same standing with the Father.

> **2 CORINTHIANS 5:21**
> **21 For he hath made him [Jesus] to be sin for us, who knew no sin; that we might be made the righteousness of God in him.**

We are the righteousness of God in Him!

Somebody said, "I'm trying to be righteous."

That's a waste of time.

Righteousness is one of the most misunderstood subjects in the church world today.

I was teaching on it once in a church in Pennsylvania. To illustrate its true meaning to the people, I suddenly stopped and said to a man on the front pew, whom the pastor had told me was the most spiritual man he'd ever pastored, "Are you righteous?"

"Well," he swallowed, "I'm trying to be."

I said, "I don't want to be vulgar, but I want to ask you a question. Are you a man, or a woman?"

"I'm a man."

"How did you get to be a man?"

"I was born that way."

"That's the way you get to be righteous," I said. "You're born that way."

Righteousness means right standing with God.

> **JOHN 15:5,8**
> **5 I am the vine, ye are the branches: He that abideth in me, and I in him, the same bringeth forth much fruit . . . .**

8 Herein is my Father glorified, that ye bear much
fruit . . . .

When you look at a tree, you don't think of the
branches as being one thing, and the main part of the tree
as being something else. It's all one tree. Jesus said, "I am
the vine, ye are the branches."

Where does the fruit grow?

On the branches! It is because of the vine life, but it is
produced out on the branches.

We should be doing the works of Christ. We are in
Christ. We have a right to use His Name to the glory of God
the Father.

"The unlimited use of the Name of Jesus," Kenyon
points out, "reveals to us the implicit confidence that God
the Father has in the Church. This in itself is a challenge."

God is a faith God. He is exhibiting His faith.

Our part is to accept the challenge.

Chapter 18

The Miraculous! Christianity's Norm

Right in the heart of Mr. Kenyon's book is a chapter entitled "Man and Miracles." It is so important I would like to cover it word for word, but I shall choose only a few quotes from it here. Again, I encourage you to get a copy of his book and to study this chapter until you grasp it.

"Jesus! The very Name has within it miracle working power, even to this day . . . Jesus' life was a miracle."

"A stream of miracles flowed from the hands of the apostles that upset Judaism and shook the Roman government to its foundation. They made a discovery—the Name of the Man Whom they had loved, Whom they had seen nailed to that cross in nakedness, now has power equal to the power that He, Himself exercised when He was among them."

"Christianity began in miracles; it is propagated by miracles. Every new birth is a miracle; every answer to prayer is a miracle; every victory over temptation is a miracle."

"When reason takes the place of the miraculous, Christianity loses its virility, fascination, and fruitfulness."

"Man craves a miracle working God today . . . Man wants a living God. Man craves a miracle."

"The answer to the universal craving of man for the supernatural is found in the new birth, and indwelling presence of the Holy Spirit, and the Name of Jesus."

"God is a miracle worker. Jesus Christ was and is a miracle. The Bible is a miracle Book . . . It is history of the outbreakings of the supernatural realm into the natural."

"When Jesus began His public ministry, it was a ministry of miracles. When the Church began her ministry, it was a ministry of miracles. Every revival since Pentecost that has honored the humble Galilean has been a revival of miracles."

"The Church has never been rescued from Her backslidings by great philosophical teachers but humble laymen who have had a new vision of the Christ, of Him Who is the same yesterday, today, and forever."

"We crave the manifest presence of the Spirit in our religious services . . . All normal men crave the supernatural—they long to see the manifestation of the power of God and to feel the thrill of the touch of the unseen."

"Man was created by a miracle working God—that miracle element is in man."

"Man yearns to perform miracles and live in the atmosphere of the supernatural."

"This miracle element in man has made him an inventor, discoverer, and investigator."

"The miracle realm is man's natural realm—he is by creation the companion of the miracle working Father-God."

The Bible says that we are *"labourers together with God"* (1 Cor. 3:9). Well, if we work together with God, we will have to be workers of miracles, because He is a miracle-working God!

"Sin dethroned man from the miracle realm, but through
grace he is coming into his own. It has been a hard struggle
for us to grasp the principles of this strange life of faith. Sin
has made us workers—grace would make us trusters."

"In the beginning, man's spirit was the dominant force in
the world; when he sinned, his mind became dominant—sin
dethroned the spirit and crowned the intellect; but grace is
restoring the spirit to its place of dominion, and when man
comes to recognize the dominance of the spirit, he will live
in the realm of the supernatural without effort. No longer
will faith be a struggle and fight, but an unconscious living
in the realm of God."

"The spiritual realm is man's normal home; it places him
where communion with God is a normal experience, where
faith in the miraculous, miracle-working God is unconscious, where he will exercise the highest type of faith
and yet be as unconscious of having exercised faith as he is
when he writes a check."

The Church's problem has been that we have lived
beneath our privileges so long, we think that is normal
Christianity. But it is abnormal. Absolutely abnormal
Christianity!

The whole Church, the Pentecostal, Full Gospel,
charismatic move included, is in a babyhood stage. We're
trying to have faith. We're trying to believe.

But, thank God, some are coming to see the light of
God's Word. And I am more convinced today than I was
yesterday, that in these last days, there is going to arise a
company of believers who will see and know their
authority, their rights and privileges in Christ. They will
know that the Name of Jesus belongs to them. They will
take up that Name and start using it as unconsciously as
they take their car keys and unlock the car door, then put
them in the ignition and start the car.

There is coming the knowledge of what was revealed all the time in the Word of God. But which we failed to see because we tried to comprehend it with human reasoning.

The Bible plainly states, *" . . . the natural man receiveth not the things of the Spirit of God: for they are foolishness unto him: neither can he know them, because they are **spiritually** discerned"* (1 Cor. 2:14).

You could read that, "the natural *mind* receiveth not the things of the Spirit of God."

Remember that the Word of God is of the Spirit of God.

> **2 PETER 1:20,21**
> **20 Knowing this first, that no prophecy of the scripture is of any private interpretation.**
> **21 For the prophecy came not in old time by the will of man: but holy men of God spake as they were moved by the Holy Ghost.**

God's Word contains God's thoughts. Those thoughts are as high above man's thoughts as the heaven is above the earth (Isa. 55:8,9).

You have to get the revelation of God's Word in your heart—your spirit. Your natural mind cannot receive the things of the Spirit of God. They are *spiritually* discerned.

The Church will never see these things unless they are preached—God put teachers in the Church to teach—but it will come, little by little. And when it comes in its fullness, and we grow out of the babyhood stage of Christianity and realize our rights and privileges, and the authority and power in that Name, and rise up to use that Name, it will be said of us as it was of the early disciples, *"These that have turned the world upside down are come hither also"* (Acts 17:6).

Chapter 19
Faith and the Name

If I just had enough faith, you might be thinking, *I could use that Name.*

You can use it anyway. It belongs to you.

If you study the Scriptures carefully, you will find that nowhere does Jesus mention faith or belief when He talks about using the Name of Jesus, except in the future tense.

Kenyon writes, "the right to use His Name is a conferred blessing to the Church: it is a Right that belongs to every child of God." Then he gives our four-fold right to use the Name.

1. We are born into the family of God and the Name belongs to the family.

2. We are baptized into the Name, and being baptized into the Name, we are baptized into Christ Himself.

3. It was conferred upon us by Jesus Who gave us the Power of Attorney.

4. We are commissioned as Ambassadors to go and herald this Name among the nations.

"I cannot see," Kenyon observes, "where we need to have any special faith to use the Name of Jesus, because it is legally ours. If I had a thousand dollars in the bank, it would not require any conscious act of faith on my part to write a check for one hundred dollars . . . .

"If you are a child of God, then you are an heir of God—a joint heir with Christ—you have a Right to the use of the Name of Jesus, and if you have this Right, it is because of your place in the family."

Faith is normal and natural to children of loving parents who provide for them. They don't worry about the next meal. They don't stop playing to come in and say, "Momma, I know that if I asked for a piece of bread you would give it to me." They automatically know that. And they act on it. They exercise an unconscious faith. No wonder Jesus said, "Except ye be converted, and become as little children, ye shall not enter into the kingdom of heaven" (Matt. 18:3). We need to get to that place of an unconscious faith in God, an unconscious faith in the Word.

Kenyon states, "I believe the hour will come when large companies of believers will live this simple life of Faith; live it unconsciously, live it daily—they will live in this upper realm where they will see in the Name of Jesus the fullness of the authority and power that was in Christ when He walked the earth."

Our problem is we have kept people in a babyhood stage of development.

One of the faults I've found with much of the teaching in recent years about discipleship, submission, etc., is that it held people babies. They couldn't develop. They couldn't make decisions. They couldn't get leadings from God for themselves. Somebody else had to tell them. That's unscriptural, unbiblical, and really unintelligent. It holds people in bondage. It holds them in a babyhood state.

God wants His children to mature—to grow up, spiritually. He wants them to be doers of the Word, and not hearers only. He wants them to begin to reign in the realm of life.

Chapter 20

Reigning by the Name

For if by one man's offence death reigned by one; much more they which receive abundance of grace and of the gift of righteousness shall reign in life by one, Jesus Christ.

—Romans 5:17

You could read that verse like this: "For if by Adam's offence spiritual death (which is the nature of Satan; which is hatred, lying, poverty, sickness) reigned by one; much more they which receive abundance of grace and of the gift of righteousness shall reign in life by one, Jesus Christ."

The *Amplified* translation, and several others, translate that, *"reign as kings in life."*

What are we to reign over? Circumstances, disease, sickness, sin, hatred—and everything else that is of the devil.

Those things will not dominate us. We will dominate them. That's what it means to reign in life.

Would you think of someone who lives on Barely-Get-Along Street, way down at the end of the block right next to Grumble Alley, who goes through life with nothing much to eat, sick, emaciated, nose-to-the-grindstone, as one who reigns in life? No, you would not.

It is when we get into the Word and think through on its truths that we actually begin to reign in life by Christ Jesus.

COLOSSIANS 1:12,13
12 Giving thanks unto the Father, which hath made us

meet to be partakers of the inheritance of the saints in light:
13 Who hath delivered us from the power of darkness, and hath translated us into the kingdom of his dear Son.

The Apostle Paul is talking about giving thanks unto God the Father for something that belongs to us right now. God has made us able to be partakers of the inheritance of the saints in light. The saints inherited something!

In verse 13 he begins to tell us about that inheritance. First, the Father God has delivered us from the power, or the authority, of darkness. That is, He has delivered us from Satan's authority. From demons. From sickness. From disease. From poverty. God has delivered us from everything that belongs to Satan.

One translation says, "He has taken us out from under the control and the dominion of darkness."

Instead of Satan's reigning over us, we are to reign over him.

Too often Spirit-filled Christians are ruled and dominated by the devil, circumstances, and everything else of this world. They ought to be happy and joyous, filled with life and light.

Let's rise up and take advantage of what belongs to us.

How is it that we're going to reign? By Christ Jesus! I think you could say it this way: We are to reign by the Name Christ Jesus. For He gave us His Name saying, "In my Name, they shall cast out demons."

Chapter 21

There Is Healing in the Name

We have had a treasure without realizing it.

You can ask people, "Does the Name of Jesus belong to the Church?"

"Yes."

"What good is it?"

"Oh, it is just to be adored and praised."

We do adore and praise the Name of Jesus, but that is not its purpose. It was given to us for our benefit.

There is healing in that Name. There must be, because Jesus said, "*In my Name*, they shall lay hands on the sick and they shall recover." There must be, because Peter said to the lame man, "Such as I have give I thee, *in the Name* of Jesus Christ of Nazareth, rise up and walk."

Full Salvation

ACTS 4:12

12 Neither is there salvation in any other: for there is none other name under heaven given among men, whereby we must be saved.

That Name of Jesus is salvation.

When we use the word "salvation"—because we have been trained that way—we automatically think of the remission of sins, the new birth. But that is only part of *salvation*. And if that is as far as you think, you limit God.

In the Scofield Reference Bible, Dr. Scofield points out the full meaning of the word *salvation* in the following footnote reference to Romans 1:16. (Romans 1:16 reads: *"For I am not ashamed of the gospel of Christ: for it is the power of God unto salvation to every one that believeth; to the Jew first, and also to the Greek.")*

> The Hebrew and Greek words for "salvation" imply the ideas of *deliverance, safety, preservation, healing* and *soundness.* Salvation is the great inclusive word of the Gospel, gathering into itself all the redemptive acts and processes.
>
> —Scofield

When God says salvation, He is talking about more than most people realize. The Gospel of Christ is the power of God unto deliverance. The Gospel of Christ is the power of God unto safety. The Gospel of Christ is the power of God unto preservation. The Gospel of Christ is the power of God unto soundness. The Gospel of Christ is the power of God unto *healing.*

When God's Word says, "There is no other name given among men whereby we must be saved," He is not just talking about the new birth. He is also talking about healing for our bodies.

There is healing in no other name.

Healing in the Redemption

We need to know that healing for our physical bodies is part and parcel of the Gospel of the Lord Jesus Christ. He not only took our sins; He also took our infirmities and bore our sicknesses.

ISAIAH 53:4,5
4 Surely he hath borne our griefs [Heb. *sicknesses*], and carried our sorrows [Heb. *pains*]: yet we did esteem him stricken, smitten of God, and afflicted.
5 But he was wounded for our transgressions, he was

bruised for our iniquities: the chastisement of our
peace was upon him; and with his stripes we are
healed.

MATTHEW 8:17
17 That it might be fulfilled which was spoken by
Esaias the prophet, saying, Himself took our infirmities, and bare our sicknesses.

1 PETER 2:24
24 Who his own self bare our sins in his own body on
the tree, that we, being dead to sins, should live unto
righteousness: by whose stripes ye were healed.

The healing that He has already provided becomes real
to us through His Name. "*In my Name*, they shall lay
hands on the sick and they shall recover." Why? Because
healing belongs to us. Jesus provided it in our redemption.

But, you see, we have been taught to divide it. We have
been taught to think like this: *The Lord does save
nowadays. The Name will work when it comes to* (what we
call) *salvation. But the Name doesn't work any further.
That's the end of it.*

No! That Name will do all it ever did! If it doesn't, then I
have no right to believe there is salvation in that Name.

Thank God, there is healing in that Name!

If we were taught concerning healing in the Name of
Jesus like we are taught in what we call salvation in the
Name of Jesus, there wouldn't be any doubt about it. We
would have an unconscious faith in healing, like we do in
the remission of sins.

The Remission of Sins

Jesus dealt with the sin problem. He *bore* our sins.
When we believe that and accept Him personally, it

becomes a reality to us individually. We are born again. We become a brand new creature—a brand new creation with no past.

> **2 CORINTHIANS 5:17**
> 17 Therefore if any man be in Christ, he is a new creature: old things are passed away; behold, all things are become new.

Old things are passed away!

The old sins that we committed before we were born again do not exist in the mind of God. He does not remember them.

> **ISAIAH 43:25**
> 25 I, even I, am he that blotteth out thy transgressions for mine own sake, and will not remember thy sins.

> **MICAH 7:19**
> 19 He will turn again, he will have compassion upon us; he will subdue our iniquities; and thou wilt cast all their sins into the depths of the sea.

If you put Isaiah 43:25 and Micah 7:19 together, you will find that God has hidden our sins in the Sea of Forgetfulness.

As Corrie ten Boom said, "Don't go fishing for them!"

Leave them alone. They don't exist anymore. God blotted them out. They do not exist in the spirit realm. Jesus bore them.

> **PSALM 103:12**
> 12 As far as the east is from the west, so far hath he removed our transgressions from us.

That distance is immeasurable! You can start

traveling east around the world, and just keep going and keep going. If you lived to be 1000 years old, and went around the world every day of that 1000 years, you still would be traveling east.

That is not the case with north and south. If you traveled north, you would one day pass the north pole and begin to travel south.

Jesus bore our sins away from us as far as the east is from the west!

Now the devil will try to remind you of them. He wants to try to hold you out of the place where the Name of Jesus will work for you. If you are under condemnation, you cannot be bold about using that Name.

He will bring a photograph before your mind of something you have done in the past.

When he does that to me, I just laugh at him and say, "Sure I did that. But all you're doing is showing me a picture of it, because God blotted it out. God dealt with that sin and put it away. He hid it in the Sea of Forgetfulness. You can't get it. You are only bringing me a picture of it."

Looking at some of the pictures he brings is rather like looking at old photographs you took several years ago. They don't look like you now. The pictures that the enemy brings are not really you! You are a new creature.

Forgiveness of Sin

But what about the sins you have committed since being born again?

1 JOHN 1:9
9 If we confess our sins, he is faithful and just to forgive us our sins, and to cleanse us from all unrighteousness.

After you become a Christian, First John 1:9 is the way to forgiveness of sins.

People often use this Scripture in dealing with sinners. But it was not written to the sinner.

A sinner could not comply with it. He couldn't confess every wrong thing he had ever done, because he couldn't remember them. His whole life is wrong.

After becoming a Christian, though, the minute you do wrong, you know it deep within your being. No one has to tell you; you know it. You can stop right then and say, "I missed it. God forgive me." And He will!

In the Name of Jesus, forgiveness of sins belongs to the Christian.

But what I want you to see is this: *It is just as easy to be healed as it is to be forgiven of your sins.*

If people would start believing that, it would work for them!

Back in the '50s, polio was rampant. A mother and her 6-year-old daughter, both victims of the disease, were brought to my meetings.

I learned later how desperate their situation was. The mother had no use of her legs and almost no use of her arms and hands. She was helpless. Someone was hired to come in part time and do the housework, but they could not afford full-time help. So while the father was at work, there were times when there was no one in the home to take care of the two polio victims.

They were not Pentecostal, but they had heard that God was healing people, and they had come in search of healing. The father pushed the wheelchair his wife was confined to down the aisle and positioned it at the front. The little girl sat in her mother's lap.

They attended several services and heard the Word

taught several times before I laid hands on them.

The little girl received her healing instantly. She jumped down off her mother's lap, and ran up and down the aisles in front of everyone.

The woman did not receive her healing.

All three were filled with the Holy Spirit and spoke with other tongues.

I said to the woman as I ministered to her, "You can receive healing for your body as easily as you received salvation. You can receive healing for your body as quickly and as easily as you received the Holy Spirit."

She said, "I wish I could believe that, Brother Hagin."

(That's what hindered her.)

I said, "You could be healed as easily as your daughter was."

She said, "I know she is healed. I wish I could be healed that easily."

She stayed in her wheelchair.

But four or five years later, I received a lengthy letter from her. Before, she could not use her hands enough to write, but she wrote this letter herself.

"Dear Brother Hagin," she began. "I wanted you to know that I am out of the wheelchair. I am walking. I have 90 percent use of my body. I will regain all of it. I'm doing all my housework. I see after our daughter. I sweep. I mop. I cook all the meals.

"I want you to know that it was the tapes I listened to sitting in that wheelchair, over and over again . . . . "

We did not have tapes at that time. But they had recorded the meetings on their own reel recorder. She had listened to them for years before the truths of God's Word on healing got into her spirit and she could receive her healing.

Many good people who are thoroughly born again have been taught only part of the Gospel. They think it all begins and ends with the new birth. It is difficult for them to believe beyond that. That's why it takes so long.

It doesn't take God a long time.

That little girl in childlike faith just accepted what was taught, and she was healed. Her mother kept sitting in the chair.

Some unbeliever might have said, "That can't be right. Why wasn't the woman healed?"

She had something to do with it.

You see, *we* have something to do with it. God has provided the remission of sins for the sinner. He has provided the forgiveness of sins for Christians. He has also provided healing for us. But we have something to do with it. And it is all wrapped up in the Name of Jesus.

God's Word is true. And we can act upon that Word.

The moment I confess my sins, He is faithful and just to forgive me my sins (1 John 1:9). The moment I confess, He forgives me. When He forgives me, I am forgiven—whether I feel like it or not; whether it seems like it or not.

"On the same ground," Kenyon says, "the moment I confess that Satan has put a disease or infirmity upon me, just that moment He [God] is faithful and righteous to heal me, and I am healed!"

Sickness comes from the same source that sin comes from. It doesn't come from heaven. There isn't any up there. Jesus told the disciples to pray, in what we call the Lord's prayer, "Thy will be done in earth as it is in heaven." Is it God's will that there be sickness in heaven? Everyone knows that it is not. Therefore it cannot be His will on earth.

Listen to Kenyon on the subject:

. . . when He gave us the right to use His Name to heal the sick, it was simply that we might bring on the scene by the use of that Name the fullness of His finished work, and that the afflicted one might know that in the use of that Name the Living, Healing Christ was present.

It is not *trying* to believe; it is not *trying* to take healing.

Believing becomes unnecessary in the modern sense of that term.

That healing is ours; that Name makes it available to us.

That Name is ours, and in that Name is all help, all victory, all power, all health.

Do not try; do not struggle—just use it.

Use that Name with the same freedom that you use your check book.

The money is on deposit; you write the check without exercising any special faith; that is, you are not conscious of exercising it—you do though.

And in the use of Jesus' Name, you do exercise Faith—it is the unconscious faith, the faith that is borne in upon us by evidences that convince us beyond the shadow of a doubt.

Any other kind of faith is abnormal.

At the Second Coming of Christ, it will not require any act of faith on our part to be translated; neither will it require any effort to receive immortality—we shall simply be made immortal—we shall be translated.

That is in the plan, in the eternal program of God.

It will not require any special faith to be resurrected—the resurrection is in the program.

But what about God's program for today? Kenyon makes this observation, "If we understand His program for today, the sick would simply be healed the moment that sickness touched them."

ROMANS 8:11
11 But if the Spirit of him that raised up Jesus from the dead dwell in you, he that raised up Christ from the

dead shall also quicken your mortal bodies by his Spirit that dwelleth in you.

This refers to our bodies now. Mortal means *death-doomed*.

Your body is the temple of the Holy Spirit only because your body is the temple of your human spirit. The Holy Spirit will not indwell your body after your human spirit has departed. The Holy Spirit will not indwell your body in the grave. He indwells your spirit now. And one of His reasons for indwelling you—not the only purpose, but one is to *quicken* your mortal body; to heal your physical body.

To quicken means to make full of life.

The only times I have been attacked in body (other than those times I violated a law of nature, such as going out into cold night air while still hot and sweaty from preaching, and not wearing a coat) were when I missed God.

I don't mean that I committed some great sin. I just wasn't obeying God exactly. I wasn't in the ministry He wanted me in; I was doing what I wanted to do. I was preaching, and what I was doing was right, but it wasn't His perfect will. So, the door was open for Satan to attack me.

Every single time, this is what happened to me when I was healed. *The Spirit of God in me quickened my mortal body.* He rose up in me.

Death came, more than once, and fastened itself upon me.

One time an Assembly of God evangelist who had been in the ministry many years was with me. (I weighed only 138 pounds and was very thin. That's why it was so easy for him to detect the beating of my heart.)

He said to me afterwards, "Brother Kenneth, I had one

hand over your heart and the other under your back as you were lying there. Your heart had stopped dead still. But when it stopped, you rose up off the bed and stood up. I never did turn loose. I held my hand on your heart as you walked the full length of this parsonage [the living room and bedroom] twice. And your heart never beat one time. The third time you started back, it began beating perfectly."

I'll tell you what happened. I didn't get up off that bed. The Spirit of God in me rose up and *quickened* my body. That power in me just lifted me up, stood me on my feet, and started me walking.

At the same time, He enlightened my mind as to where I had missed it. I had pushed my body. (Our bodies are still mortal. We cannot overwork without our bodies' reacting.) I had overworked, gotten too hot, and had something like a heat stroke.

As I turned to walk the length of that parsonage the third time, while the power of God held me, I promised God, "I'll never push my body that far again."

The minute I promised Him, my heart started beating.

Another time, death came and fastened its final throes upon me. (I know; I've been dead twice.) I had missed God, gotten out of His will, and the devil attacked me. The death chill was upon my brow.

Yet the minute that happened, on the inside of me (the Holy Spirit dwells in you) He rose up and *quickened* my body. Life went all over my body.

The Lord said to me once in the winter of '48 (and I didn't fully understand what He was saying until now), "I did not put gifts of healings and the Name of Jesus in the Church for the Church to heal themselves with. I put the Name of Jesus and the gifts of healings in the Church for the Church to heal the world with."

You see, the Church ought to walk in Romans 8:11!

Listen again to Kenyon:

> . . . one of the reasons of His indwelling is to heal our
> physical bodies of the diseases that are continually
> attaching themselves to us.
>
> When we understand this, we shall not be *trying* to
> exercise faith for our healing, or for any other need—we
> shall simply recognize the fact that this healing, this need,
> is in the program, is a part of it, and we shall accept what
> belongs to us . . . .
>
> He bore our sins in His body on the tree and He died
> because of those sins, and we believe that we died with
> Him—then we do not have to die again to sin.
>
> He was made alive, and we were made alive with Him.

In Ephesians we see that word *quickened* again.
Remember that it means to be made alive.

> **EPHESIANS 2:1,5,6**
> **1 And you hath he quickened, who were dead in
> trespasses and sins . . . .**
> **5 Even when we were dead in sins, hath quickened
> us together with Christ, (by grace ye are saved;)**
> **6 And hath raised us up together, and made us sit
> together in heavenly places in Christ Jesus.**

We died to sin in Christ. We were quickened (made
alive) with Him. We died to our sins. We died to our old
nature. We also died to our diseases. We arose in the
fullness of His life. That is what full salvation is.

> As we come to understand this, we know that our old sin
> nature hasn't any right, any privilege, to reign over us
> because it is dead, and we will not accept any imitation of it
> that Satan may in our ignorance impose upon us, neither

will we recognize any condemnation that might come to us through any sins we may have committed in the past, for Christ bore them, and we need never bear them again, neither do we need to suffer any condemnation for them because He was condemned for them, and He bore them.

Consequently, we are free, and there is, "therefore, now, no condemnation to us because we are in Christ Jesus."

The same thing is true with our sicknesses. Isaiah 53:4 "He bore our sicknesses and carried our pains." (correct translation)

Now, sickness hasn't any right to impose itself upon us and Satan hasn't any right to impose any diseases upon us.

We are free!

And when these diseases and sicknesses come, all we need to do is treat them exactly the same as we treat our old sins.

—Kenyon

I have not had one sick day in 45 years. I did not say that the devil hadn't attacked me. But before the day is out, I am healed.

When the devil does attack, I say to him, "Satan, those diseases were borne in the body of Jesus. You have no right to bring their photograph around here to frighten me with. Now you just pick up your things, pack them up, and get out of here. I will not accept it."

Someone else says, "I'm taking a cold."

That's a mistake. They accepted it.

Jesus put away sin. He "bare" our sins. He also "took" our infirmities, and "bare" our sicknesses.

The Greek and Hebrew words translated "bare" mean "to remove or convey to a distance."

That sickness is not there. Satan is trying to bring it to me. If I will accept it, he can put it on me. But I won't accept it because Jesus did something about it.

This profound statement by Kenyon sums it up:

There is no more need of our bearing about in our bodies our sicknesses than there is of bearing about in our spiritual nature an unforgiven sin.

Chapter 22

Confession and the Name

Confession holds an important place in connection with the Name of Jesus. We should confess our faith in Jesus as a person, but we should also confess our faith in the Name of Jesus.

I saw this as a Baptist boy 45 years ago. I saw Mark 11:23 and 24. And I began to say out loud—I confessed with my mouth—what I believed in my heart, and within the hour the paralysis disappeared, the heart trouble was gone, the incurable blood disease was gone. I was well. And I'm still well.

Some Christians oppose themselves. They say, "I don't believe in that confession business."

I love them. I'm not against them; I'm for them. I feel so sorry for them, I could weep about it. But if there is nothing to that confession business, then there is nothing to salvation.

> **ROMANS 10:9,10**
> 9 That if thou shalt CONFESS with thy mouth the Lord Jesus, and shalt believe in thine heart that God hath raised him from the dead, thou shalt be saved.
> 10 For with the heart man believeth unto righteousness; and with the mouth CONFESSION is made unto salvation.

There is no salvation without confession. There is no remission of sin, no new birth, without confession.

Our Christian experience begins with confession.

The trouble with the church world in general is, they started and stopped right there. They stopped at the starting place—and it has held them in the babyhood stage of spiritual development.

Christianity is called "our confession."

HEBREWS 3:1
1 Wherefore, holy brethren, partakers of the heavenly calling, consider the Apostle and High Priest of our profession [confession], Christ Jesus.

The word the King James translates *profession* here is the same Greek word translated *confession* in Romans 10:9 and 10.

W. E. Vine's *Expository Dictionary of New Testament Words* gives this meaning for it: to declare openly by way of speaking out freely, such confession being the effect of deep conviction of facts. Kenyon points out that it means "witnessing a confession of our lips."

People may not realize what they are saying when they say it, but to say, "I don't believe in confession," is tantamount to saying, "I don't believe in Christianity."

We see the place confession holds in the new birth experience. It holds the same place in our daily walk. For the Christian's daily walk is a walk of faith (2 Cor. 5:7).

HEBREWS 4:14
14 Seeing then that we have a great high priest, that is passed into the heavens, Jesus the Son of God, let us hold fast our profession [confession].

Christianity is a confession.

Let us hold fast to the witnessing and confession of our lips.

Let us hold fast to saying who we are, what we are, and what we have, because we are in Christ.

Let us hold fast to the confession of our place in Christ—to the confession of our rights and privileges in Christ Jesus—to the confession of what God the Father has done for us in Christ, and to what the Spirit through the Word of God has done in us and is able to do through us.

Our faith is measured by our confession. We can never realize beyond our confession.

The Name of Jesus will work for us when we begin to confess what that Name will do.

Kenyon points out a danger, however:

> There is a grave danger of our having two confessions.
> One would be the integrity of the Word, and the other would be of our doubts and fears.

To confess the integrity of the Word of God, and then to turn around and confess doubts and fears will build confusion into our spirits.

If God's Word is true—and it is—and if we believe in the integrity of God's Word, doubt and fear can have no place with us. They have to go.

Someone said, "When faith comes in the front door, doubt goes out the back door. When faith comes in the front door, fear goes out the back." You cannot have both faith and doubt. You cannot have faith and fear.

I remember the struggle I had in learning to hold fast to my confession. I hadn't read any books on the subject—I wish I had; it would have helped me immeasurably.

After I was raised up and healed, I went back to high school. I was over 6 feet tall and weighed 89 pounds. They called me a walking skeleton.

One doctor on my case asked my aunt, "Is that boy up?"

"Yes."

He said, "I saw him in town the other day, and thought I was seeing a ghost. I believe that boy has the strongest will power of any person I've ever seen. But he won't be up long. I'll give him 90 days at the most to live."

I walked a mile and a half to school. I went up and down

staircases to my classes. Naturally, I was weak. Heart symptoms began to come back on me.

The principal called me to his office.

He said, "Kenneth, do you suppose you ought to come to school? The lady teachers in particular are afraid you're going to fall dead in their classrooms."

One of them had called the doctor. He'd told her, "I don't know how he's made it. He's up by sheer will power. He cannot live. Climbing those steps with the condition his heart is in, he could keel over dead at any moment. You may look up in the classroom, and he'll be dead at his desk."

That really helped those ladies!

So the principal said to me, "Education is fine. I'm an educator. But your health comes first. Should you come to school?"

I said, "Sir, I am not up by will power." Now I was far from being Spirit-filled, but I'd caught a glimpse of the truth. I said (I made my confession), "I am not up by will power. I am up by faith. And my faith will hold."

The heart symptoms did come back on me. But I never told anyone.

I struggled with it in the nighttime. There was no one to help me. Anyone I might talk to, would talk me out of it. I didn't know everything I know now. But I remember how at exactly 4 o'clock one morning, I saw I was making two confessions.

You see, you can make wrong confessions to yourself.

I was saying, "Yes, according to the Word of God my faith will work. According to God's Word I'm healed."

But I was also saying, "Yes, I've got heart symptoms. In fact, if it gets any worse, I don't know what I'm going to do."

The second confession nullified the first.

So, that morning at 4 o'clock I cut off the second one.

I wouldn't even say to myself, "I've got heart symptoms."

I would say to myself (I went to sleep confessing it), "According to His Word I am healed." I would give the Scripture, chapter, and verse for it.

I was attending a convention being held in a large church when a pastor we all knew suffered a heart attack. The doctors told his wife he would never regain consciousness. She knew the convention was in progress, so she rushed out of the hospital room to a telephone and called us to pray.

Raymond T. Richey, a noted healing preacher, was there. They called him to the platform to lead in prayer.

He said, "Let's all lift our hands and pray for the healing of Brother S."

We lifted our hands and prayed in Jesus' Name that the man would live and not die. Two thousand of us prayed at once. The sound was tremendous. After a while, we began to quieten down, one by one, until all were quiet.

Mr. Richey said, "How many of you believe God heard us?"

I lifted my hand. At least 90 percent of the crowd lifted their hands.

"Let's lift our hands and praise God for the answer," Richey said.

We all praised God a few moments for the man's healing. Mr. Richey walked off the platform. The song leader began leading a song.

Then Brother Richey—I will never forget it, because I was standing close by—suddenly whirled around and ran up the steps to the pulpit. He put his arm around the song

leader and said something to him. The fellow stopped
singing. Everyone stopped. Everyone was quiet.

Raymond T. Richey said, "How many of you are going
to keep on praying for Brother S?"

I didn't raise my hand. I wasn't going to pray anymore.
I was going to praise God for the answer because I believe
the Name of Jesus works. But I looked around, and I'm
sure 90 percent of the crowd lifted their hands.

Brother Richey said, "What for? I thought you already
believed God heard you?"

The whole crowd missed what he said. Preachers
standing around me blinked their eyes and said, "What is
he talking about?"

They missed it. They were living in another realm.

Several years later I heard the man we were praying
for tell how as he lay unconscious in the hospital a few
blocks away from where we held the convention, suddenly
Jesus appeared by his bed, looked at him, and said, "I am
the Lord that healeth thee." He rose up well.

Somebody might have said, "Oh, that great convention
and all those thousands of people praying got the job
done."

No. It was Brother Richey and I, and maybe one or two
others. If that man had been depending on the crowd, he
would have died. Because if they kept on praying, they
would have nullified the effects of their prayers!

> Every time we confess weakness and failure and doubt
> and fear, we go to the level of them.
>
> We may pray very ardently and very earnestly and
> declare in our prayers our faith in the Word and yet, the
> next moment we question whether He heard us or not, for
> we confess we have not the things for which we prayed.
>
> Our last confession destroys our prayer.
>
> —Kenyon

So many prayers have been destroyed. Christians are good at it. And most of the time they don't know what they are doing.

People often come up to me after a service and ask me to pray for their healing. I lay my hand on them, pray and claim it, and thank God for it. For the Word of God says, "In the Name of Jesus . . . they shall lay hands on the sick and they shall recover."

Then I boldly declare, "It's done in the Name of Jesus. You will recover. Glory to God. I believe it."

Many times they say, "Brother Hagin, I want you to keep on praying for me."

I say, "What for?"

"Well," they say, "for my healing."

I say, "It won't do any good. You've just denied the Word of God. You've just denied that you are going to recover, because you want to keep on praying."

You see, I prayed the prayer of faith. But by their confession they nullified my prayer and destroyed the effects of my faith.

The Name of Jesus and faith in that Name always works! It is possible, though, for someone else to nullify the effects of your prayer.

Some of our RHEMA Bible Training Center students asked me about the death of a relative. They said, "Brother Hagin, we laid hands on him. We prayed for him. We had all the faith in the world, but he died. Where did we fail?"

I said, "You didn't fail. God heard you."

You see, the other person can nullify the effects of my faith. I would let them cut off my head before I would say that God didn't hear me. He heard me when I prayed. If someone does die, God still heard me. And He sent the answer. They did not receive it.

I spent many hours praying at the bedside of a returned missionary. He was eaten up with cancer throughout his body. Only 37 years old, he was helpless, the picture of death.

One day I had been praying for about two and a half hours. Suddenly, about a foot away from the foot of the bed, Jesus appeared. He wore a white robe. I saw Him as plainly as I ever saw anyone.

I didn't tell the missionary that I saw Jesus, but I did say to him, "Jesus has come to heal you."

(The healing was already bought nearly 2000 years ago, but Jesus so wanted the man to be healed that He came in person to manifest the healing.)

When I said that, the man did something he was incapable of doing. He leaped out of bed, ran down to the foot of the bed, and stood right in front of Jesus, facing Him.

(He told me later, after I had told him I saw Jesus, "I didn't see Him, but He stood right there, didn't He? I sensed His Presence." A Presence stood there as real as a man would stand there.)

It seemed that Jesus held something in His hands like you would hold a bowl. It must have been the man's healing. It was an oddly shaped *something*. He held it out to the man.

The man reached out his hands to take it. Then he dropped them, dropped his head, and a frown came over his face. He stepped back. He sat down on a stool at the foot of the bed, put his head in his hands and said, "I can't. I can't. I can't."

I said, "You can't what?"

He said, "I can't receive my healing."

I said, "Yes, you can. You can receive your healing.

Jesus has come to heal you."

He stood up and stepped toward Jesus. He stood right in front of Him.

Jesus reached out to hand something to him.

He reached out his hands to take it. (He never saw anything, but he sensed it in the spirit.) Then his hands fell to his side. The frown came over his face. He backed back to the stool and sat down, put his head into his hands, and cried with tears, "I can't. I can't. I can't."

I said, "You can't what?"

He said, "I can't receive it. I just can't receive my healing."

I said, "Yes, you can. Jesus has come to heal you."

He stood the third time, stepped up a couple of steps, reached out his hands, and Jesus reached out to hand him what I knew was his healing. But again he dropped his hands, backed back, sat on the stool, dropped his head into his hands, and said, "I can't. I can't receive my healing."

I will never forget it. I could have reached out and touched Jesus as He said to me with a tone of sadness in His voice, "See, I've come to heal him, and he won't let me. Now, he will be dead in (so-many) days."

And he was.

Was that the will of God?

No! I'm glad he went to heaven. I'm glad he's up there now, shouting up and down the streets of gold. But I'm so sorry he missed out on what he should have had in this life. He ought to have been back on the mission field.

Was it God's will to heal him?

Did God hear my prayer?

Yes. I prayed the prayer of faith and Jesus, in a supernatural manifestation, came to deliver the healing Himself.

What nullified the effects of the prayer of faith?
The man's unbelief.

God always hears me. (When you know it, He hears you.) I came in Jesus' Name. He said to me, and He cannot lie, "Whatever you ask the Father in my Name, He will give it you." You cannot make a stronger assertion than "I will" or "He will." *He will give it you.*

People substitute their thinking for Bible thinking when they say, "Well, if you pray the prayer of faith for me, it will work whether I have any faith or not."

That's erroneous, unscriptural thinking.

"If you pray the prayer of faith for me, it will work whether I'm living right or wrong."

No, it won't.

The Bible plainly states, *"Can two walk together, except they be agreed?"* (Amos 3:3). They cannot.

My confession is, "He always hears me!" He heard me on the part of that 37-year-old missionary. But that dear man annulled my prayer; he destroyed the effects of my faith.

How? By wrong confession.

Your confession must absolutely agree with the Word. When you have prayed in Jesus' Name, you are to hold fast your confession. Do not destroy the effects of your own prayer by a negative confession.

We have included some confessions here. Say these aloud with your mouth because you believe them in your heart.

Confession

The Name of Jesus is above all names.
The Name of Jesus is greater than every name.

The Name of Jesus has authority
  in heaven, in the earth, under the earth.
The Name of Jesus has authority at the throne of God.
The Name of Jesus gives me authority
  over the demons of hell.
The Name of Jesus belongs to me today, in the earth.
For if two of you shall agree on earth as touching any thing
  that they shall ask, it shall be done for them of my Father
  which is in heaven.
For where two or three of you are gathered together
  in my Name, I am there.
Jesus is here.
He's here to see that my prayer is heard and answered.
He's here to honor what I say—for "If you ask anything
  in my Name, I will do it."
His Name has authority.
He has authorized me to use that Name
  against my enemies—all of hell, all demons,
  sickness and disease, and sin as well—
  oppression and depression.
So, in the Name of Jesus, I am free.
I declare my freedom today.
For Jesus has set me free.
And all that He's done, and all of His power,
  and all of His authority, and the might of all His
  conquests, are invested in the Name.
And that Name belongs to me!
I'm more than a conqueror through Him that loved me
  and gave Himself for me.
So I take the Name and I walk victoriously.

Chapter 23

Scriptures for Meditation

You can learn a lot by looking up every Scripture in the New Testament in relation to His Name.

It's enlightening. It's thrilling. It's enthralling. It's faith-building. It's instructive.

Faith comes by hearing, and hearing by the Word of God (Romans 10:17). Without meditation in the Word of God on the subject of the Name of Jesus, you will not have the faith in it you should have. It will not work, even though you purport to believe in it.

For instance, you believed in the Name of Jesus before you read this book. But through the teaching, your faith in that Name has grown stronger. Your confidence, your assurance, your respect for that Name has grown stronger.

Take time to meditate on all the Scriptures in the New Testament concerning that Name.

Take time to look up every Scripture in the New Testament relative to His Name.

We have included some of them here.

In the Book of Acts you will come face to face with the fact that the early church must have devoted time to instructing people in regard to the use of the Name of Jesus. They must have understood that they had what we call "the power of attorney" or, the legal right to the use of the Name of Jesus.

Jesus gave that to them.

But He didn't give it just to them. He gave it to the whole Church. That means He gave it to us.

I think this is what has happened: The devil has blinded our eyes to the truth because of church teaching that was not scriptural.

People did not take time to examine the Scriptures for

themselves. They were taught things such as this: "The apostles had that kind of power. They could heal the sick and so on to get the Church established. But when the last apostle died, then all that ceased."

Therefore, generally speaking, the Church thought that ceased, so no effort to study or learn about those things was made. The people thought, "That was for them then."

But when one begins to study the Scriptures in detail for himself, he is confronted with facts that raise some questions to such teaching.

If the healings and miracles were wrought in the Name of Jesus—and no intelligent person could deny it—and they are not for us today, then the Name of Jesus is not for us now. If the Name of Jesus is not for us now, then no one is saved, for there is salvation in no other name. And if His Name only works when it comes to the new birth, then that Name has lost half its power, Jesus is diminishing, God is growing smaller, the Church is growing weaker, and the devil is growing bigger.

That is not what the Bible teaches!

If we think these things through, we cannot accept conclusions such as, it all stopped with the last apostle.

The problem with most has been, they were not thinking.

I am not willing to let the other person do my thinking for me. I did a lot of thinking when I was bedfast 45 years ago. And I began to see things in the Bible that my church didn't teach. Though I was just a teenager, I decided, *I am not going to let my church do my thinking for me. I am going to accept God's Word for what it says.*

The Gospels

MATTHEW 1:21
21 And she shall bring forth a son, and thou shalt call
his name JESUS: for he shall save his people from
their sins.

MATTHEW 1:23
23 Behold, a virgin shall be with child, and shall bring
forth a son, and they shall call his name Emmanuel,
which being interpreted is, God with us.

MATTHEW 1:24,25
24 Then Joseph being raised from sleep did as the
angel of the Lord had bidden him, and took unto him
his wife:
25 And knew her not till she had brought forth her
firstborn son: and he called his name JESUS.

MATTHEW 10:22
22 And ye shall be hated of all men for my name's sake:
but he that endureth to the end shall be saved.

MATTHEW 12:18,21
18 Behold my servant, whom I have chosen; my
beloved, in whom my soul is well pleased: I will put my
spirit upon him, and he shall shew judgment to the
Gentiles . . .
21 And in his name shall the Gentiles trust.

MATTHEW 18:5
5   And whoso shall receive one such little child in my
name receiveth me.

MATTHEW 18:19,20
19 Again I say unto you, That if two of you shall agree
on earth as touching any thing that they shall ask, it
shall be done for them of my Father which is in
heaven.

20 For where two or three are gathered together in my name, there am I in the midst of them.

MATTHEW 19:29
29 And every one that hath forsaken houses, or brethren, or sisters, or father, or mother, or wife, or children, or lands, for my name's sake, shall receive an hundredfold, and shall inherit everlasting life.

MATTHEW 28:19
19 Go ye therefore, and teach all nations, baptizing them in the name of the Father, and of the Son, and of the Holy Ghost.

MARK 9:38-41
38 And John answered him, saying, Master, we saw one casting out devils in thy name, and he followeth not us: and we forbad him, because he followeth not us.
39 But Jesus said, Forbid him not: for there is no man which shall do a miracle in my name, that can lightly speak evil of me.
40 For he that is not against us is on our part.
41 For whosoever shall give you a cup of water to drink in my name, because ye belong to Christ, verily I say unto you, he shall not lose his reward.

MARK 16:17,18
17 And these signs shall follow them that believe; In my name shall they cast out devils; they shall speak with new tongues;
18 They shall take up serpents; and if they drink any deadly thing, it shall not hurt them; they shall lay hands on the sick, and they shall recover.

LUKE 10:17
17 And the seventy returned again with joy, saying, Lord, even the devils are subject unto us through thy name.

LUKE 24:46,47
46 . . . Thus it is written, and thus it behoved Christ to suffer, and to rise from the dead the third day:
47 And that repentance and remission of sins should be preached in his name among all nations, beginning at Jerusalem.

JOHN 1:12
12 But as many as received him, to them gave he power to become the sons of God, even to them that believe on his name.

JOHN 2:23
23 Now when he was in Jerusalem at the passover, in the feast day, many believed in his name, when they saw the miracles which he did.

JOHN 3:18
18 He that believeth on him is not condemned: but he that believeth not is condemned already, because he hath not believed in the name of the only begotten Son of God.

JOHN 14:13,14
13 And whatsoever ye shall ask in my name, that will I do, that the Father may be glorified in the Son.
14 If ye shall ask any thing in my name, I will do it.

JOHN 14:26
26 But the Comforter, which is the Holy Ghost, whom the Father will send in my name, he shall teach you all things, and bring all things to your remembrance, whatsoever I have said unto you.

JOHN 15:16
16 Ye have not chosen me, but I have chosen you, and ordained you, that ye should go and bring forth fruit, and that your fruit should remain: that whatsoever ye shall ask of the Father in my name, he may give it you.

JOHN 15:20,21

20 ... If they have persecuted me, they will also persecute you; if they have kept my saying, they will keep yours also.

21 But all these things will they do unto you for my name's sake, because they know not him that sent me.

JOHN 16:23,24,26

23 And in that day ye shall ask me nothing. Verily, verily, I say unto you, Whatsoever ye shall ask the Father in my name, he will give it you.

24 Hitherto have ye asked nothing in my name: ask, and ye shall receive, that your joy may be full ....

26 At that day ye shall ask in my name ....

JOHN 20:31

31 But these are written, that ye might believe that Jesus is the Christ, the Son of God; and that believing ye might have life through his name.

The Acts

ACTS 2:21

21 And it shall come to pass, that whosoever shall call on the name of the Lord shall be saved.

ACTS 2:38

38 Then Peter said unto them, Repent, and be baptized every one of you in the name of Jesus Christ for the remission of sins, and ye shall receive the gift of the Holy Ghost.

ACTS 3:6

6 Then Peter said, Silver and gold have I none; but such as I have give I thee: In the name of Jesus Christ of Nazareth rise up and walk.

ACTS 3:16
16 And his name through faith in his name hath made
this man strong, whom ye see and know: yea, the faith
which is by him hath given him this perfect soundness
in the presence of you all.

ACTS 4:7,8,10,12,17,18
7 And when they had set them in the midst, they
asked, By what power, or by what name, have ye done
this?
8 Then Peter, filled with the Holy Ghost,
said . . . .
10 Be it known unto you all, and to all the people of
Israel, that by the name of Jesus Christ of Nazareth,
whom ye crucified, whom God raised from the dead,
even by him doth this man stand here before you
whole.
12 Neither is there salvation in any other: for there is
none other name under heaven given among men,
whereby we must be saved . . . .
17 But that it spread no further among the people, let
us straitly threaten them, that they speak henceforth
to no man in this name.
18 And they called them, and commanded them not to
speak at all nor teach in the name of Jesus.

ACTS 4:29,30
29 And now, Lord, behold their threatenings: and
grant unto thy servants, that with all boldness they
may speak thy word,
30 By stretching forth thine hand to heal; and that
signs and wonders may be done by the name of thy
holy child Jesus.

ACTS 5:28,40-42
28 . . . Did not we straitly command you that ye should
not teach in this name? and, behold, ye have filled
Jerusalem with your doctrine, and intend to bring this

man's blood upon us . . . .

40 . . . and when they had called the apostles, and beaten them, they commanded that they should not speak in the name of Jesus, and let them go.

41 And they departed from the presence of the council, rejoicing that they were counted worthy to suffer shame for his name.

42 And daily in the temple, and in every house, they ceased not to teach and preach Jesus Christ.

ACTS 8:12

12 But when they believed Philip preaching the things concerning the kingdom of God, and the name of Jesus Christ, they were baptized, both men and women.

ACTS 9:14-16

14 And here he [Saul/Paul] hath authority from the chief priests to bind all that call on thy name.

15 But the Lord said unto him, Go thy way: for he is a chosen vessel unto me, to bear my name before the Gentiles, and kings, and the children of Israel:

16 For I will shew him how great things he must suffer for my name's sake.

ACTS 9:21,27,29

21 But all that heard him [Paul] were amazed, and said; Is not this he that destroyed them which called on this name in Jerusalem . . . .

27 But Barnabas took him, and brought him to the apostles, and declared unto them how he had seen the Lord in the way, and that he had spoken to him, and how he had preached boldly at Damascus in the name of Jesus . . . .

29 And he spake boldly in the name of the Lord Jesus, and disputed against the Grecians . . . .

ACTS 10:43

43 To him give all the prophets witness, that through

his name whosoever believeth in him shall receive remission of sins.

ACTS 10:48
48 And he commanded them to be baptized in the name of the Lord. Then prayed they him to tarry certain days.

ACTS 15:25,26
25 It seemed good unto us, being assembled with one accord, to send chosen men unto you with our beloved Barnabas and Paul,
26 Men that have hazarded their lives for the name of our Lord Jesus Christ.

ACTS 16:18
18 And this did she many days. But Paul, being grieved, turned and said to the spirit, I command thee in the name of Jesus Christ to come out of her. And he came out the same hour.

ACTS 19:5
5 When they heard this, they were baptized in the name of the Lord Jesus.

The Epistles

ROMANS 1:5
5 By whom we have received grace and apostleship, for obedience to the faith among all nations, for his name.

ROMANS 10:13
13 For whosoever shall call upon the name of the Lord shall be saved.

1 CORINTHIANS 1:2
2 Unto the church of God which is at Corinth, to them

that are sanctified in Christ Jesus, called to be saints, with all that in every place call upon the name of Jesus Christ our Lord, both theirs and ours.

1 CORINTHIANS 1:10
10 Now I beseech you, brethren, by the name of our Lord Jesus Christ, that ye all speak the same thing, and that there be no divisions among you; but that ye be perfectly joined together in the same mind and in the same judgment.

1 CORINTHIANS 6:11
11 And such were some of you: but ye are washed, but ye are sanctified, but ye are justified in the name of the Lord Jesus, and by the Spirit of our God.

EPHESIANS 5:20
20 Giving thanks always for all things unto God and the Father in the name of our Lord Jesus Christ.

PHILIPPIANS 2:9,10,11
9 Wherefore God also hath highly exalted him, and given him a name which is above every name:
10 That at the name of Jesus every knee should bow, of things in heaven, and things in earth, and things under the earth;
11 And that every tongue should confess that Jesus Christ is Lord, to the glory of God the Father.

COLOSSIANS 3:17
17 And whatsoever ye do in word or deed, do all in the name of the Lord Jesus, giving thanks to God and the Father by him.

2 THESSALONIANS 1:12
12 That the name of our Lord Jesus Christ may be glorified in you, and ye in him, according to the grace of our God and the Lord Jesus Christ.

2 TIMOTHY 2:19
19 Nevertheless the foundation of God standeth sure, having this seal, The Lord knoweth them that are his. And, Let every one that nameth the name of Christ depart from iniquity.

HEBREWS 1:4
4 Being made so much better than the angels, as he hath by inheritance obtained a more excellent name than they.

HEBREWS 6:10
10 For God is not unrighteous to forget your work and labour of love, which ye have shewed toward his name, in that ye have ministered to the saints, and do minister.

HEBREWS 13:15
15 By him therefore let us offer the sacrifice of praise to God continually, that is, the fruit of our lips giving thanks to his name.

JAMES 5:14
14 Is any sick among you? let him call for the elders of the church; and let them pray over him, anointing him with oil in the name of the Lord.

1 PETER 4:14
14 If ye be reproached for the name of Christ, happy are ye; for the spirit of glory and of God resteth upon you: on their part he is evil spoken of, but on your part he is glorified.

1 JOHN 2:12
12 I write unto you, little children, because your sins are forgiven you for his name's sake.

1 JOHN 3:23
23 And this is his commandment, That we should

believe on the name of his Son Jesus Christ, and love one another, as he gave us commandment.

1 JOHN 5:13
13 These things have I written unto you that believe on the name of the Son of God; that ye may know that ye have eternal life, and that ye may believe on the name of the Son of God.

REVELATION 19:12,13,16
12 His eyes were as a flame of fire, and on his head were many crowns; and he had a name written, that no man knew, but he himself.
13 And he was clothed with a vesture dipped in blood: and his name is called The Word of God . . . .
16 And he hath on his vesture and on his thigh a name written, KING OF KINGS, AND LORD OF LORDS.

REVELATION 22:3,4
3   And there shall be no more curse: but the throne of God and of the Lamb shall be in it; and his servants shall serve him:
4   And they shall see his face; and his name shall be in their foreheads.

The following prophetic utterance came through tongues and interpretation as Kenneth E. Hagin taught "The Name of Jesus" seminar in April 1978:

But, yea, come ye, saith the Lord,
  with an open heart,
  and a mind that is receptive to My Word;
And the truth of the Word of God
  shall dawn upon your spirit.
And ye shall realize that you are thoroughly furnished,
  with all that you need,
To meet the enemy in combat from day to day.

And so, thou shalt be victorious,
Not just once in a while,
But every single day of thy life.
For thou shalt put the enemy to flight.
And thou shalt enjoy victory in every fight.

But some would say, "Oh, that sounds too good to be true.
I've tried before to walk in the light
  of what I thought was God's Word.
And it just won't work for me.
  I just don't know what's wrong."

Yea, saith the Lord,
Humble thyself before Me and My Word,
And acknowledge with all sincerity,
"Thy Word is truth, and I will stand upon thy Word;
  And I will speak forth thy Word;
  And I will pick up that Name,

  With all of its authority, and majesty, excellence, and glory;

Even the Name that's above every Name.
Because that Name is mine;
And from this day forward, I will refuse to relent;
I will refuse to be defeated;
But I will stand my ground and enjoy the fullness
of all the blessing that belongeth unto me."

Yea, saith the Lord,
Learn all that belongs unto you.
Study to know, and the Spirit of the Lord
will unto you show the mightiness of His glory,
the greatness of His authority, the reality of His presence.
And you shall stand in His Name,
And it will be a strong tower unto thee
For protection against all the storms of life
And the onslaughts of the enemy
And all that the enemy shall seek to do unto you.
You need not cry out in fear,
And cry out in desperation,
Even though sometimes because of the lack of knowledge,
He will hear.
But in all calmness and peace,
And serenity of heart and mind,
Ye can say, "The Truth I do find.
Yea, I've found the way of life and truth.
I've found the way of majesty, royalty, and goodness.
For Jesus has overcome,
And His Name, with all of its majesty and glory
Today is the same.
I will exercise my rights
And walk in the light
Of His Word."